THE COOK'S ENCYCLOPEDIA OF
FOUR INGREDIENT
COOKING

THE COOK'S ENCYCLOPEDIA OF
FOUR INGREDIENT COOKING

JOANNA FARROW

BARNES
&NOBLE
BOOKS
NEW YORK

This edition published by Barnes & Noble, Inc.,
by arrangement with Anness Publishing Limited

2003 Barnes & Noble Books

M 10 9 8 7 6 5 4 3

ISBN 0-7607-3828-9

© Anness Publishing Limited 2003
Hermes House
88-89 Blackfriars Road
London SE1 8HA

Publisher: Joanna Lorenz
Managing Editor: Linda Fraser
Senior Editor: Susannah Blake
Copy Editor: Bridget Jones
Editorial Reader: Richard McGinlay
Production Controller: Steve Lang
Photography: Tim Auty, Martin Brigdale, Nicky Dowey, Gus Filgate, Michelle Garrett,
Amanda Heywood, William Lingwood, Craig Robertson, Simon Smith
Recipes: Alex Barker, Jacqueline Clark, Joanna Farrow, Brian Glover, Jane Milton,
Jennie Shapter, Marlena Spieler, Kate Whiteman

Also published as *Take Four*

NOTES

Standard spoon and cup measures are level.

Large eggs are used unless otherwise stated.

The very young, elderly and those in ill-health or with a compromised immune system
are advised against consuming raw eggs or dishes containing raw eggs.

Contents

The Minimalist Approach

In recent years, cooking and eating trends have changed considerably, with more emphasis on dishes that are quick and easy to prepare, yet that are still exciting, sophisticated, and delicious. This book teaches you how to really make the most of food—with simple, fabulous recipes that use only four ingredients, or fewer. Using a limited number of top-quality ingredients allows you to really savor the aroma, taste, and texture of a dish and saves time on writing lists and shopping for ingredients. It also allows for fuss-free preparation, giving you more time to sit back, relax, and enjoy.

When you're cooking with four ingredients, each one has to be a star player. It is important to buy the best quality ingredients you can find, so be selective when buying, as the better the raw materials, the more flavor the finished dish will have. Top-quality produce will also need fewer additional seasonings or flavorings to make them taste fabulous. Buying the best does not necessarily mean paying more. For example meat from a good, traditional-style butcher is often cheaper than the better-quality types in the supermarket and it will probably have a fuller flavor. Good fish can be slightly harder to find. Be particularly choosy when buying from supermarket fish counters: Avoid tired-looking specimens and remember that it is better to go for good-quality frozen fish and shellfish rather than poor-quality fresh. Farmers' market stores can be great sources of good-quality fruit and vegetables, often at a good price, even for the more exotic produce.

Ready-made stocks and sauces are infinitely useful for creating quick and easy meals and are a great way to cut down on preparation and cooking time. A basic tomato sauce can lay the foundations for hundreds of different dishes, such as stews, casseroles, and pasta dishes. Simply add poultry, meat, fish, vegetables, or legumes and flavor with fresh herbs and spices. Sauces, such as pesto, are great for adding flavor, while a really great ready-made custard can be the perfect base for an ice cream. Good-quality bought sauces are readily available fresh or in jars—check out the list of ingredients on the pack for some indication of the quality. A good bought liquid concentrate or fresh stock is worth keeping in the refrigerator or freezer. Remember that many bought chilled fresh products are suitable for home freezing, which is a good way of extending their shelf life. Alternatively, you can make your own supply of basic stocks and sauces and freeze them in practical, ready-to-use batches.

Choosing really fresh, good-quality ingredients will help you to create delicious, flavorsome dishes.

Fresh herbs go perfectly with other simple flavors and play an essential role in minimalist cooking.

Adding a splash of robust wine or herb-steeped vinegar to a sauce or stew can help to give extra body and flavor.

Pantry essentials

Try to keep the pantry to a minimum. Choose good-quality extra virgin olive oil and balsamic vinegar for dressings and a lighter oil, such as sunflower or safflower. oil for cooking. A nut oil, such as walnut or hazelnut, makes an interesting alternative to olive oil in salad dressings. One or two flavored oils are great for adding extra taste.

Preserved or dried vegetables, such as sun-dried tomatoes, bottled roasted bell peppers, and capers, have a powerful flavor and can be useful for boosting flavor in many Mediterranean-style dishes. Dried mushrooms bring a full flavor to mushroom dishes and can be good for perking up simple soups, stews, casseroles, and risottos.

Keep herb and spice supplies to a minimum as both lose their flavor comparatively quickly, particularly if exposed to light and warmth. If possible, it is better to grow or buy fresh herbs and freeze any leftovers for future use rather than stocking a pantry full of dried spices that have an inferior flavor. If possible, stock whole spices, such as cumin and coriander, and grind them using a mortar and pestle or in a spice grinder as required, as ground spices tend to lose their flavor quickly. Freshly grated whole nutmeg is better than ready ground and it adds interest to potato dishes and white sauces.

Other essential pantry ingredients include salt and ground black pepper, sugar, all-purpose flour, and cornstarch, plus staples, such as pasta and rice. It is also handy to have a selection of condiments or sauces, such as soy sauce or pesto, that can perk up or enhance the flavor of simple dishes.

Rich-tasting anchovies are a perfect ingredient to keep in the pantry.

Using the recipes

Each recipe uses no more than four ingredients, excluding salt, pepper, and water. Some recipes use ready-made stock or sauce—but you can always use a homemade one if you like. Serving suggestions and ideas for garnishes or decorations are included where appropriate, but these are not essential for the success of the dish. There are also suggestions for variations that offer alternative or additional flavorings and handy cook's tips that will help you achieve successful results every time.

Equipment

Having the right equipment makes cooking both easier and more enjoyable; chopping ingredients with a blunt knife simply becomes laborious. There is very little essential equipment and many so-called labor-saving gadgets are, more often than not, used once or twice and then put away, cluttering up useful storage space. Knives, pans, mixing bowls, wooden spoons, roasting and baking pans, measuring cups, whisks, and strainers are all essential and the following are some items to which it is worth paying special attention.

Knives

Always buy good-quality knives. Although they are quite expensive, they will last for years, so buy them as you can afford them to build up a small set. Store knives in a knife rack or case for safety and to protect the blades. Blades should be sharpened frequently for good performance.

A good-quality knife is essential for preparing ingredients.

Cutting board

When chopping meat or fish, always use a plastic board and scrub well after use. However, a large, heavy sturdy wooden board is a good choice for preparing vegetables and fruit as it will not slip while in use. Avoid glass boards as they blunt knives very quickly.

Pans

Three or four different-sized pans are ample for most households. Choose heavy pans, as they do not burn easily when making sauces and long-simmered dishes.

Skillets

One large, heavy stainless steel skillet, preferably with a lid, is sufficient in most kitchens. However, a nonstick pan is essential for dry-frying foods or for cooking in a very small amount of oil.

Wok

Even if you do not do much stir-frying or Asian-style cooking, a wok is useful for a variety of other cooking methods, such as cooking and tossing pasta dishes, vegetables, tomato sauces, and any other ingredients that might normally spill out of a traditional skillet.

Measuring spoons

A set of metal measuring spoons and is essential, as table cutlery can vary widely in volume, making spoons intended for eating or serving food unsuitable for measuring . Sets usually include $\frac{1}{4}$, $\frac{1}{2}$, and 1 teaspoon, plus 1 tablespoon. Some sets also include a dessertspoon, which is equal to 2 teaspoons, and/or $1\frac{1}{2}$ tablespoons. When measuring dry ingredients, heap the spoon, then level it with the back of a knife blade.

A set of measuring spoons is a small, worthwhile investment.

Measuring cups

Heatproof cups marked with fractions of a cup are useful for measuring liquids. Plastic cups, which may vary in size from $\frac{1}{4}$–1 cup, may be used to measure wet and dry ingredients.

Electrical equipment

Food processors are the most useful of all the electrical appliances, as they take the effort out of chopping, blending, grating, and making

A goblet blender is perfect for making drinks and soups.

pastes. Some large food processors have smaller containers that fit inside the large bowl for processing smaller quantities. A blender wand or hand-held blender that processes ingredients in a pan is especially useful and, like a goblet blender, it reduces soups to a finer texture than a food processor. An electric whisk is practical for whipping cream, creaming cake mixtures, and whisking egg whites.

Cooking techniques

Allowing onions to brown, caramelizes their surface and adds flavor to the final dish.

When using a limited number of ingredients, straightforward, flavor-enhancing cooking methods are the best choice. Frying, broiling, and roasting can help to enrich the ingredients, causing caramelization and browning on the surface. The cooked food will be well flavored, needing little more than lemon wedges or a simple condiment to complete the dish. Steaming is quite different—highlighting the natural flavor of ingredients. Minimum seasonings are necessary, but subtle sauces can enhance the plain cooked foods. Concentrating on simple cooking methods helps to keep the core recipe quick and easy to prepare.

Frying

This is good for enriching the natural flavor of ingredients. There are several methods: deep-frying, pan-frying or shallow-frying, stir-frying, and dry-frying. Each one uses different quantities of fat and produces different results.

The initial frying of ingredients can help to determine the final character of a dish. Heat the oil before adding the ingredients and do not add too much to the pan at once. Overfilling the pan will steam or braise, rather than fry the food, which will affect the final flavor. If necessary, fry ingredients in batches. Stir-frying uses less oil than traditional frying methods and combines all the ingredients in one pan, bringing together a few complementary flavors. The juices yielded in stir-frying are usually sufficient to form a sauce. Dry-frying in a nonstick pan requires no fat, so is ideal when trying to reduce the number of cooking ingredients.

Deep-frying can bring out rich flavors in simple ingredients.

Broiling

Cooking under a broiler or on a griddle can really bring out the flavor of good-quality ingredients, imparting a rich, smoky flavor. Meat, poultry, fish, shellfish, and vegetables need little more than light seasoning and brushing with oil. Time permitting, the food can be marinated in advance in a bought marinade or simple mixture of lemon juice or wine,

Cooking on a griddle is quick and easy and produces delicious, attractive results.

garlic, and herbs. Preheat the broiler before cooking the food and baste non-fatty foods with oil, marinade, or a basting mixture to prevent them from drying out.

Roasting

Traditionally appreciated for cooking meat and poultry, roasting is also excellent for large pieces of fish and vegetables. The ingredients are cooked uncovered to encourage browning and the formation of a crisp and golden surface. When temperature and timing are correct, the foods stay moist and succulent inside. Basting with butter or olive oil, or

Chicken is delicious roasted with simple aromatic flavors, such as garlic and herbs.

juices that seep out during cooking, helps to flavor and crisp the skin as well as keep the food moist.

Steaming

This simple cooking method focuses on the natural, raw, taste of the food. Cooking in steam does not impart flavor in the way that frying, broiling, and roasting can, so it is best used for cooking ingredients that have an excellent natural flavor, which can be savored plain or served with an interesting sauce or accompaniment. Steaming is a gentle method that produces wonderfully moist results and is perfectly suited to vegetables and fish. Check food frequently during steaming, as some foods cook surprisingly quickly.

Making Basic Stocks

A well-flavored stock is particularly good in dishes that rely on minimal ingredients. Good-quality ready-made stocks—either bouillon cubes or powders or liquid concentrate—are readily available, but they are easy and cheap to make. Always ask for the meat bones when buying from a butcher and trimmings if you have fish prepared at a fish store, as these are perfect for making good stock. A chicken carcass from a roast makes excellent stock, particularly if you've packed it with herbs, onions, garlic, or other aromatics before roasting. A good vegetable stock can be made from trimmings when preparing vegetables and small quantities of leftover produce. Leave the onion skins on if you want a rich, dark-colored stock.

Beef Stock   MAKES ABOUT 4 CUPS

2 pounds beef bones

2 unpeeled onions, cut into fourths

1 bouquet garni

2 large carrots, coarsely chopped

1 Preheat the oven to 425°F. Put the beef bones in a roasting pan and roast for about 45 minutes, or until well browned.

2 Transfer the roasted bones to a large, heavy pan. Add the onion fourths, leaving the skins on, the bouquet garni, and chopped carrots. Add 1 teaspoon salt and 1 teaspoon black peppercorns. Pour over about 7½ cups cold water and bring just to a boil.

3 Using a slotted spoon, skim off any scum on the surface of the stock. Reduce the heat and partially cover the pan. Simmer the stock on the lowest heat for about 3 hours, then set aside to cool slightly.

4 Strain the stock into a large bowl and let cool completely, then remove any fat from the surface. Store the stock in the refrigerator for up to 3 days or freeze for up to 6 months.

Chicken Stock   MAKES ABOUT 4 CUPS

1 large roast chicken carcass

2 unpeeled onions, cut into fourths

3 bay leaves

2 large carrots, coarsely chopped

1 Put the chicken carcass and any loose bones and roasting juices into a heavy pan in which they fit snugly. Add the onion fourths, bay leaves, and chopped carrots.

2 Add ½ teaspoon salt and 1 teaspoon black peppercorns to the pan, and pour over 7½ cups cold water. Bring just to a boil.

3 Reduce the heat, partially cover the pan, and cook on the lowest setting for about 1½ hours. Using a large spoon, carefully turn the chicken in the stock and crush the carcass occasionally.

4 Let the stock cool slightly, then strain into a large bowl, and let cool completely. When it is cool, remove any fat from the surface and discard. Store the stock in the refrigerator for up to 2 days or freeze for up to 6 months.

Fish Stock

1¼ pounds fish bones and trimmings, without heads and gills

1 bouquet garni

1 onion or 3–4 shallots, peeled and cut into fourths

2 celery stalks, coarsely chopped

1 Pack the fish bones and trimmings into a heavy pan and add the bouquet garni, onion or shallots, and celery.

2 Add ½ teaspoon salt and ½ teaspoon peppercorns to the pan and pour over 4 cups water. Bring to a boil.

3 Reduce the heat, partially cover the pan, and cook on the lowest setting for about 30 minutes, stirring occasionally. Let cool slightly, then strain into a bowl, and let cool completely. Store in the refrigerator for up to 24 hours or freeze for up to 3 months.

Vegetable Stock

3 unpeeled onions, cut into fourths

7 ounces large open mushrooms

10–14 ounces mixed vegetables, such as broccoli, carrots, celery, zucchini, tomatoes, and/or scallions, coarsely chopped

3 tablespoons green or brown lentils

1 Place the onions in a heavy pan with the mushrooms, mixed vegetables, and green or brown lentils.

2 Add ½ teaspoon salt, 2 teaspoons peppercorns, and 7½ cups water to the pan. Bring to a boil, then reduce the heat, and simmer, partially covered, for 50–60 minutes.

3 Let the stock cool slightly, then strain into a bowl, and let cool completely. Store in the refrigerator for up to 24 hours or freeze for up to 6 months.

Bouquet Garni

This little bundle of herbs is perfect for adding flavor to stocks, soups, and stews. Tying the herbs in a bundle means that the bouquet garni is easy to remove after cooking. A traditional bouquet garni comprises sprigs of parsley, thyme, and a bay leaf, but you can vary the herbs according to the dish and/or main ingredients. Rosemary and oregano are good with lamb, or mint, chervil, basil, chives, and tarragon go well with fish.

1 Using a short length of string, tie together a bay leaf and sprigs of thyme and parsley.

2 Alternatively, place the herbs in the center of a small square of cheesecloth and tie into a neat bundle using a short length of string.

3 Use the bouquet garni immediately or freeze, ready for cooking. (Herbs tied in cheesecloth are better suited to freezing than bundles simply tied with string.)

FREEZING STOCK

The main ingredients for stock can be frozen—meat bones, fish trimmings, or a cooked chicken carcass—ready for making homemade stock at a later date.

More conveniently, stock itself freezes very well. Once the stock has been strained and the fat removed, reduce the volume by boiling the stock uncovered. This concentrates its flavor and takes up less freezer space. A highly reduced stock, boiled to a thick syrup, can be frozen in an ice cube tray. Make a note of the volume before boiling, then add this to the label when packing the stock for the freezer. This way you will know how much water to add when the concentrated stock is thawed.

Making Basic Savory Sauces

A good sauce can provide the finishing touch for a dish. There is a large number of ready-made sauces available, but they are also very easy to make yourself. One of the most basic sauces is the classic savory white sauce, which can be served as a simple topping for vegetables or flavored with additional ingredients, such as cheese, herbs, onions, or mushrooms, and served with pasta, fish, or poultry. A basic fresh tomato sauce is widely used for pasta dishes, pizza toppings, and vegetable dishes and it is worth making when ripe tomatoes are available. It can be stored in the refrigerator for several days or can be frozen for up to 6 months. Hollandaise sauce is another classic accompaniment for fish and vegetables. Unlike the other sauces, it cannot be made ahead, but it it is available commercially.

White Sauce MAKES ABOUT 1¾ CUPS

1¼ cups milk

1 tablespoon butter

2 tablespoons all-purpose flour

freshly grated nutmeg

1 Warm the milk in a small pan. In a separate pan, melt the butter over gently heat, then add the flour, and cook, stirring, for 1 minute, until the mixture forms a thick paste.

2 Remove the pan from the heat and gradually add the warmed milk, whisking constantly until smooth.

3 Return the pan to gentle heat and cook, whisking, until the sauce boils, is smooth and thickened. Season with salt and freshly ground pepper and plenty of nutmeg.

Fresh Tomato Sauce MAKES ABOUT 4 CUPS

3 pounds ripe tomatoes

½ cup garlic-steeped olive oil

1 large onion, finely chopped

small handful of basil leaves, torn, or 2 tablespoons chopped fresh oregano

1 Put the tomatoes in a bowl, pour over boiling water to cover, and let stand for about 1 minute until the skins split. Drain and peel, then coarsely chop the flesh.

2 Heat half the oil in a large, heavy pan. Add the chopped onion and cook gently for about 3 minutes, or until softened but not browned.

3 Add the tomatoes and the remaining oil to the pan and cook gently, stirring, for 5 minutes, or until the tomatoes are soft and juicy.

4 Add the herbs, cover, and cook gently for 20–25 minutes, stirring frequently, until the sauce is thickened and pulpy. Season to taste.

VARIATIONS

• *Try using different herbs, such as flat leaf parsley, marjoram, thyme, rosemary, or cilantro in place of the basil or oregano.*

• *To make a mildly peppery sauce, add a little paprika or, to make a spicy sauce, add a little chili powder (or a finely chopped fresh chile).*

• *To make a much more garlicky sauce, add 2–3 crushed garlic cloves to the pan just before adding the chopped tomatoes.*

Hollandaise Sauce ½ CUP

3 tablespoons white wine or herb-steeped vinegar

1 bay leaf

2 egg yolks

½ cup butter, chilled

1 Put the white wine or herb vinegar in a small pan with the bay leaf and add 1 teaspoon black peppercorns. Boil rapidly until reduced to 1 teaspoon, then strain into a heatproof bowl.

2 Put the vinegar in a clean pan, add the egg yolks and a little salt and whisk lightly until thoroughly combined. Cut the chilled butter into small pieces.

3 Add the butter to the pan and set the pan over a very low heat. Whisk continuously so that as the butter melts it is blended into the egg yolks. When all the butter has melted, continue whisking until the sauce is thick and smooth.

4 Season the sauce with salt and ground black pepper to taste, adding a few extra drops of vinegar, if you like, to give a slightly tangy flavor. Serve warm.

Mayonnaise MAKES ⅔ CUP

1 egg yolk, at room temperature

1 tablespoon lemon juice or white wine vinegar

1 teaspoon Dijon mustard

⅔ cup olive oil

1 Put the egg yolk in a bowl with the lemon juice or vinegar, mustard, and a little salt. Whisk together until combined.

2 Gradually add the oil in a thin trickle, whisking constantly until the sauce is thickened and smooth. This will take several minutes.

3 Check the seasoning, adding a few drops of lemon juice or white wine vinegar if the mayonnaise is too bland. If the sauce is too thick, stir in a few drops of warm water or light cream. Cover and store in the refrigerator for up to 2 days.

Flavored Oils

There are plenty of flavored oils available in delicatessens and supermarkets, steeped with aromatics, such as lemon, garlic, herbs, and chiles, which are delicious served as a simple dressing for freshly cooked pasta or a salad. Homemade versions are less expensive and you can be more selective with the flavors you choose. Once made, the oil should be left in a cool place for up to a week to let the flavors steep. Then the oil should be strained before storing. The aromatic ingredients should not be stored long term in the oil, because of the risk of harmful molds developing.

Basil Oil Blend a large handful of basil leaves with scant 1 cup olive oil in a food processor. Leave overnight, then strain through a cheesecloth-lined strainer into a clean bowl. Store in the refrigerator, then bring to room temperature before using.

Garlic and Rosemary Oil Put a handful of rosemary sprigs in a pan with 3 sliced garlic cloves and ½ cup olive oil. Heat gently until bubbling, then pour into a heatproof bowl, cover, and leave in a cool place overnight. Strain the garlic and rosemary oil into a clean 1¼–1⅔ cup bottle and top up with more oil.

Making Basic Sweet Sauces

From creamy, comforting custard to an elegant fruit coulis, sweet sauces can be used to uplift the simplest desserts to create a truly spectacular dish. They can be served as an accompaniment or make up an intrinsic part of a dish. Simple vanilla ice cream is taken to new levels when served with hot chocolate sauce or a fresh raspberry coulis, while a classic vanilla custard can be used as the base of a sweet soufflé. These sweet sauces rely on just a few basic ingredients and minimal effort inevitably produces irresistible results. The dessert sauce can be made in advance, before serving the meal, ready for reheating or serving cold. Even custard can be reheated, just take care to use very gentle heat to prevent it from curdling.

Real Custard 1¼ CUPS

1¼ cups whole milk or half milk and half heavy cream

3 egg yolks

1 teaspoon cornstarch

3 tablespoons superfine sugar or vanilla sugar

1 Pour the milk or milk and cream mixture into a double boiler or a heavy pan and gradually bring to a boil over very gentle heat.

2 Meanwhile, whisk the egg yolks with the cornstarch and sugar until thoroughly mixed. Pour the boiled milk into the yolk mixture, whisking constantly until combined.

3 Pour the mixture back into the cleaned pan and cook over the lowest heat, stirring constantly with a wooden spoon, for 8–10 minutes, or until the mixture coats the back of the spoon.

4 Immediately pour the custard through a strainer into a bowl or pitcher to prevent it from overcooking. Serve warm.

COOK'S TIP
Always cook custard over the lowest heat possible to reduce the risk of curdling. Adding a little cornstarch to the sauce helps to prevent it from curdling without affecting the consistency or flavor.

Summer Fruit Coulis MAKES ABOUT 1 CUP

¾ cup raspberries

generous 1 cup strawberries

2–3 teaspoons confectioners' sugar

1 tablespoon orange liqueur or kirsch (optional)

1 Place the raspberries and strawberries in a food processor and process until smooth. Press the mixture through a fine strainer set over a bowl to remove the tiny seeds.

2 Return the strained fruit purée to the food processor or blender and add 2 teaspoons of the confectioners' sugar with the orange liqueur or kirsch, if using, and process briefly until well combined.

3 Check the sweetness of the coulis, then add a little more confectioners' sugar if necessary and process again to mix.

Rich Chocolate Sauce MAKES ABOUT 1 CUP

⅔ cup superfine sugar

6 ounces semisweet chocolate, broken into pieces

2 tablespoons sweet butter

2 tablespoons brandy or coffee liqueur (optional)

1 Put the sugar in a small, heavy pan with ½ cup water and heat gently until the sugar dissolves. Bring to a boil and boil for 1 minute.

2 Remove from the heat and stir in the chocolate and butter, stirring until the chocolate has melted and the sauce is smooth.

3 Stir in the brandy or coffee liqueur, if using, and serve warm.

Rosemary and Almond Cream MAKES ABOUT 2½ CUPS

This deliciously fragrant cream is more of an accompaniment than a sauce and is an excellent alternative to plain whipped cream served with fruit compotes, pies, and tarts, or a bowl of fresh fruits. Rosemary works really well (particularly if you then decorate the dish with flowering sprigs), but bay leaves or thyme sprigs also provide a lovely flavor.

1¼ cups heavy cream

2 fresh rosemary sprigs

½ cup finely ground amaretti or macaroon cookies

1 tablespoon almond liqueur, such as amaretto (optional)

1 Pour the heavy cream into a pan, then add the rosemary sprigs, and heat gently until the cream bubbles. Let the mixture cool, then strain into a bowl.

2 Add the finely ground cookies to the flavored cream and add 1 tablespoon almond liqueur, if you like.

3 Whisk the cream and crushed cookies together until the mixture is just holding its shape, then transfer to a serving dish, and chill until ready to serve.

Flavored Sugar

A store of herb-and spice-steeped sugars provides plenty of flavoring options for sauces, desserts, and cakes without the need for additional ingredients. Vanilla sugar is the best known and can be bought easily, but there are many other equally useful flavors. Use in any recipe instead of ordinary sugar or use half flavored and half ordinary sugar.

Vanilla Sugar Half fill a small storage jar with white or golden superfine sugar and add 1 vanilla bean. Top off with sugar, seal, and store in a cool place for a week before using.

Spice Sugar Half fill a small storage jar with superfine sugar and add either 2 broken cinnamon sticks; 1 tablespoon lightly bruised cardamom pods, or 4 star anise, and top off with more sugar. Seal and store in a cool dark place for about a week before using.

Flower or Herb Sugar Half fill a small storage jar with superfine sugar and add either a handful of fresh, dry rose petals; several sprigs of lavender, rosemary, or thyme; or several bay leaves. Shake gently to distribute the flowers or herbs and top off with more sugar, seal, and store in a cool dark place for about a week before using.

Juices and Drinks

FRESHLY MADE FRUIT AND VEGETABLE JUICES CAN ACT AS
A REFRESHING, REVITALIZING TONIC, WHILE FROTHY HOT
CHOCOLATE OR VANILLA CAFFÈ LATTE CAN BE A RELAXING,
INDULGENT TREAT. THIS CHAPTER IS PACKED WITH EASY-
TO-MAKE DRINKS THAT CAN BE SIPPED AT LEISURE OR
ENJOYED AS A PICK-ME-UP WHEN SPIRITS ARE FLAGGING.

Leafy Apple Lift-off

This delicious blend of fruit and fresh green leaves is refreshing and healthy. The leaves are robustly flavored and have a peppery, pungent taste. To prepare the leaves, discard any damaged and discolored ones and rinse thoroughly in cold water to remove any grit. To prevent the juice from being watery, dry the leaves in a salad spinner or on paper towels before juicing.

SERVES ONE

1 Cut the apple into fourths. Using a juice extractor, juice the fruit and watercress, arugula, or spinach.

2 Add the lime juice to the apple, grape, and leaf mixture and stir thoroughly to blend all the ingredients together. Pour the juice into a tall glass and serve immediately.

1 eating apple

5 ounces white grapes

1 ounce watercress, arugula, or spinach

1 tablespoon lime juice

Fennel Fusion

The hearty combination of raw vegetables and apples makes a surprisingly delicious juice that is packed with natural goodness and is a truly wonderful pick-me-up. Use the remaining cabbage and fennel to make a really crunchy salad—slice and dress with French dressing or simply with olive oil, herb vinegar, and plenty of freshly ground black pepper and sea salt to taste.

SERVES ONE

1 Coarsely slice the red cabbage and the fennel bulb and cut the eating apples into fourths. Using a juice extractor, juice the vegetables and fruit.

2 Add the lemon juice to the red cabbage, fennel, and apple mixture and stir thoroughly to blend all the ingredients together. Pour into a glass and serve immediately.

½ small red cabbage

½ fennel bulb

2 eating apples

1 tablespoon lemon juice

Tropical Calm

This deliciously scented juice is packed with goodness to cleanse and calm the system. Orange fruits, such as cantaloupe melons and papayas, are rich in the phytochemical betacarotene, which is a valuable anti-oxidant and is thought to have many health-promoting properties.

SERVES ONE

1 papaya

½ cantaloupe melon

3½ ounces seedless white grapes

1 Halve the papaya, remove the seeds and skin, then cut the flesh into coarse slices. Halve the melon, remove the seeds, cut into fourths, slice the flesh away from the skin, and cut into chunks.

2 Using a juicer, juice the prepared fruit. Alternatively, blend the fruit in a food processor or blender for a thicker juice. Serve immediately.

Strawberry Soother

Relax with this comforting blend of just two fruits—it is rich in vitamin C and fabulous flavor. It's a perfect drink for summer when sweet strawberries, peaches, and necatarines are in season.

SERVES ONE

2 cups strawberries

1 peach or nectarine

1 Hull the strawberries. Using a sharp knife, cut the peach or nectarine into fourths and pull out the pit. Cut the flesh into coarse slices or chunks.

2 Using a juice extractor, juice the fruit. Alternatively, place the fruit in a food processor or blender and process until smooth. Serve immediately.

Carrot Revitalizer

This vibrant combination of vegetables and fruit makes a lively, health-giving drink. Carrots yield generous quantities of sweet juice, which goes perfectly with the sharp flavor of pear and the zesty taste of orange. This powerful drink will nourish and stimulate the system.

SERVES ONE

1 Scrub and trim the carrots and cut the apples into fourths. Peel the orange and cut into coarse segments.

2 Using a juice extractor, juice the carrots and fruit, pour into a glass, and serve immediately.

3 carrots

2 apples

1 orange

Purple Pep

Jewel-colored beet juice is well known for its detoxifying properties so this juice makes the perfect choice when you've been overdoing it. It offers an excellent supply of valuable nutrients that are essential for good health.

SERVES ONE

3 carrots

4 ounces beet

1 ounce baby spinach, washed and dried

2 celery stalks

1 Scrub and trim the carrots and beet. Using a sharp knife, cut the beet into large chunks.

2 Using a juice extractor, juice the carrots, beet, spinach, and celery, then pour into a glass, and serve immediately.

Melon Pick-me-up

Spicy fresh ginger root is delicious with melon and pear in this reviving and invigorating concoction. Charentais melon can be used instead of the cantaloupe melon in this recipe. To enjoy fresh ginger root at its best and most pungent, buy it in small quantities, and keep in a cool, dry place for up to a week. As it ages, the root will dry out and become hard.

SERVES ONE

1 Cut the cantaloupe melon into fourths, remove the seeds using a teaspoon or a sharp knife, and carefully slice the flesh away from the skin, reserving any juice. Cut the pears into fourths and reserve any juice.

2 Using a juice extractor, juice the melon flesh and juice, the pear fourths and juice, and the fresh ginger root. Pour the juice into a tall glass and serve immediately.

½ cantaloupe melon

2 pears

1-inch piece of fresh ginger root

Apple Shiner

This refreshing fusion of sweet apple, honeydew melon, red grapes, and lemon provides a reviving burst of energy and a feel-good sensation. Serve as a drink or use to pour over granola for a quick and healthy breakfast.

SERVES ONE

1 eating apple

½ honeydew melon

3½ ounces red grapes

1 tablespoon lemon juice

1 Cut the apple into fourths and remove the core. Cut the melon into fourths, remove the seeds, and slice the flesh away from the skin.

2 Using a juice extractor, juice the apple, melon, and grapes. Alternatively, process the fruit in a food processor or blender for 2–3 minutes, until smooth. Pour the juice into a long, tall glass, stir in the lemon juice, and serve immediately.

Citrus Sparkle

Zesty citrus fruits are packed with vitamin C, which is necessary for a healthy immune system. Pink grapefruit have a sweeter flavor than the yellow varieties—in fact, the pinker they are, the sweeter they are likely to be. For a lighter drink to serve two, divide the juice among two glasses, and top off with sparkling water or club soda and ice.

SERVES ONE

1 Cut the pink grapefruit and orange in half and squeeze out the juice using a citrus fruit squeezer.

2 Pour the juice into a glass, stir in 1 tablespoon lemon juice, add the remaining lemon juice, if required, and serve immediately.

1 pink grapefruit

1 orange

2 tablespoons freshly squeezed lemon juice

Hum-zinger

Aromatic tropical fruits make a drink that is bursting with flavor and energy. Enjoy a glass first thing in the morning to kick-start your day.

SERVES ONE

½ pineapple, peeled

1 small mango, peeled and pitted

½ small papaya, seeded and peeled

1 Remove any "eyes" left in the pineapple, then cut all the fruit into fairly coarse chunks.

2 Using a juice extractor, juice the fruit. Alternatively, process in a food processor or blender for about 2–3 minutes, until smooth. Pour into a glass and serve immediately.

Honey and Watermelon Tonic

This refreshing juice will help to cool the body, calm the digestion, and cleanse the system, and may even have aphrodisiac qualities. On hot days add ice to keep the juice cool. The distinctive pinkish-red flesh of the watermelon gives this tonic a beautiful hue—decorate with a few fresh mint leaves to provide a stunning color contrast.

SERVES FOUR

1 Cut the watermelon flesh into chunks, cutting away the skin and discarding the black seeds. Place in a large bowl, pour the chilled water over it, and let stand for 10 minutes.

2 Tip the mixture into a large strainer set over a bowl. Using a wooden spoon, press gently on the fruit to extract all the liquid.

3 Stir in the lime juice and sweeten to taste with honey. Pour into a pitcher or glasses and serve.

1 watermelon

4 cups chilled spring water

juice of 2 limes

honey, to taste

Cranberry, Ginger, and Cinnamon Spritzer

Partially freezing fruit juice gives it a refreshingly slushy texture. The combination of cranberry and apple juice is sharp and clean. Add a few fresh or frozen cranberries to decorate each glass, if you like.

2½ cups chilled cranberry juice

⅔ cup clear apple juice

4 cinnamon sticks

about 1⅔ cups chilled ginger ale

SERVES FOUR

1 Pour the cranberry juice into a shallow freezerproof container and freeze for about 2 hours, or until a thick layer of ice crystals has formed around the edges.

2 Mash the semifrozen juice with a fork to break up the ice, then return the mixture to the freezer for 2–3 hours more, or until it is almost solid.

3 Pour the apple juice into a small pan, add two cinnamon sticks, and bring to just below boiling point. Pour into a pitcher and let cool, then remove the cinnamon sticks, and set them aside. Cool, then chill the juice.

4 Spoon the cranberry ice into a food processor or blender. Add the cinnamon-flavored apple juice, and process briefly until slushy. Pile the mixture into cocktail glasses, top off with chilled ginger ale, decorate with cinnamon sticks, and serve immediately.

Strawberry and Banana Smoothie

The blend of perfectly ripe bananas and strawberries creates a drink that is both fruity and creamy, with a luscious texture. Papaya, mango, or pineapple can be used instead of strawberries for a tropical drink. Popular with adults and children alike, this is a great way to get children to enjoy fruit—much healthier than commercial milkshakes, too.

SERVES FOUR

1¾ cups strawberries, plus extra, sliced, to decorate

2 ripe bananas

1¼ cups skim milk

10 ice cubes

1 Hull the strawberries. Peel the bananas and chop them into fairly large chunks.

2 Put the fruit in a food processor or blender. Process to a thick, coarse purée, scraping down the sides of the goblet as necessary.

3 Add the skim milk and ice cubes, crushing the ice first unless you have a heavy-duty processor. Process until smooth and thick. Pour into tall glasses and top each with strawberry slices to decorate. Serve immediately.

EXTRAS *For a rich and velvety drink, add ½ cup coconut milk and process as above. In this case, reduce the volume of skim milk to ¾ cup.*

Raspberry and Orange Smoothie

Sharp-sweet raspberries and zesty oranges taste fabulous combined with the light creaminess of yogurt. This smoothie takes just minutes to prepare, making it perfect for breakfast—or any other time of the day. If you like a really tangy drink, add freshly squeezed lemon or lime juice to taste.

SERVES TWO TO THREE

1 Place the raspberries and yogurt in a food processor or blender and process for about 1 minute, until smooth and creamy.

2 Add the orange juice to the raspberry and yogurt mixture and process for about 30 seconds, or until thoroughly combined. Pour into tall glasses and serve the smoothie immediately.

1½ cups fresh raspberries, chilled

scant 1 cup plain yogurt, chilled

1¼ cups freshly squeezed orange juice, chilled

COOK'S TIP *For a super-chilled version, use frozen raspberries or a combination of frozen summer berries, such as strawberries, red currants, and blueberries, instead of fresh. You may need to process the raspberries and yogurt slightly longer for a really smooth result.*

New York Egg Cream

No one knows precisely why this legendary drink is called egg cream, but some say it was a witty way of describing richness at a time when no one could afford to put both expensive eggs and cream together in a drink. Use whole milk for a really creamy taste. Dust a little unsweetened cocoa powder over the top of the egg cream before serving, if you like.

SERVES ONE

3–4 tablespoons good quality chocolate syrup

½ cup chilled milk

¾ cup chilled sparkling water

1 Carefully pour the chocolate syrup into the base of a tall glass, avoiding dripping any on the inside of the glass.

2 Pour the chilled milk into the glass onto the chocolate syrup.

3 Gradually pour the chilled sparkling water into the glass, sip up any foam that rises to the top of the glass, and carefully continue to add the remaining chilled sparkling water. Stir thoroughly before drinking.

COOK'S TIP *A truly authentic egg cream is made using an old-fashioned seltzer dispenser that you press and spritz. In any case, you can use bottled club soda, rather than sparkling water, if you like.*

Banana and Maple Flip

This satisfying drink is packed with so much goodness that it makes a complete breakfast in a glass—great for when you're in a hurry. Be sure to use a really farm-fresh egg. The glass can be decorated with a slice of orange or lime to serve.

SERVES ONE

1 small banana, peeled and halved

¼ cup thick strained plain yogurt

1 egg

2 tablespoons maple syrup

1 Put the peeled and halved banana, thick strained plain yogurt, egg, and maple syrup in a food processor or blender. Add 2 tablespoons chilled water.

2 Process the ingredients constantly for about 2 minutes, or until the mixture turns a really pale, creamy color and has a nice frothy texture.

3 Pour the banana and maple flip into a tall, chilled glass and serve immediately. Decorate the glasses with an orange or lime slice, if you like.

COOK'S TIPS

• To chill the drinking glass quickly, place it in the freezer while you are preparing the drink.

• For a hint of sharpness, add 1 teaspoon lemon or lime juice, or use a slightly tangy yogurt.

Atole

This drink, rather like a thick milkshake in consistency, is made from Mexican cornmeal (masa harina) and flavored with piloncillo (Mexican unrefined brown sugar). Ground cinnamon and/or fresh fruit purées are often added before serving, and some recipes introduce ground almonds.

SERVES SIX

1 Combine the milk with 2½ cups cold water. Put the masa harina in a heavy pan and gradually beat in the milk and water mixture to make a smooth paste.

2 Place the pan over medium heat, add the vanilla bean, and bring the mixture to a boil, stirring constantly until it thickens. Beat in the sugar and stir until dissolved. Remove from the heat, discard the vanilla bean and serve immediately.

2½ cups milk

1¾ cups white masa harina

1 vanilla bean

¼ cup piloncillo or soft dark brown sugar

EXTRAS

Process 1 cup strawberries, chopped pineapple, or orange segments in a food processor or blender until smooth,, then press the purée through a strainer. Stir the purée into the corn mixture and return the pan to the heat until warmed through. Remove the vanilla and serve.

Café de Olla

This spiced black coffee is one of the most popular drinks in Mexico. The name means out of the pot, which refers to the heavy earthenware cooking pot, or *olla*, in which the coffee is made. Piloncillo is the local unrefined brown sugar, but any soft dark brown sugar can be used. French or Viennese roast coffees work particularly well in this hot drink.

SERVES FOUR

½ cup piloncillo or soft dark brown sugar

4 cinnamon sticks, each about 6 inches long

⅔ cup freshly ground coffee, from dark-roast coffee beans

1 Pour 4 cups water into a pan. Add the sugar and cinnamon sticks. Heat gently, stirring occasionally to make sure that the sugar dissolves, then bring to a boil. Boil rapidly for about 20 minutes, until the syrup has reduced by a fourth.

2 Add the ground coffee to the syrup and stir well, then bring the liquid back to a boil. Remove from the heat, cover the pan, and let stand for about 5 minutes.

3 Strain the coffee through a fine strainer. Pour into cups and serve.

Vanilla Caffè Latte

This luxurious vanilla and chocolate version of the classic coffee drink can be served at any time of the day topped with whipped cream, with cinnamon sticks to stir and flavor the drink. Caffè latte is a popular breakfast drink in Italy and France, and is now widely available elsewhere.

SERVES TWO

1 Pour the milk into a small pan and bring to a boil, then remove the pan from the heat. Mix the espresso or very strong coffee with 2 cups of the boiled milk in a large heatproof pitcher. Sweeten with vanilla sugar to taste.

2 Return the remaining boiled milk in the pan to the heat and add the 3 tablespoons vanilla sugar. Stir constantly until dissolved. Bring to a boil, then reduce the heat. Add the bittersweet chocolate and continue to heat, stirring constantly until all the chocolate has melted and the mixture is smooth and glossy.

3 Pour the chocolate milk into the pitcher of coffee and whisk thoroughly. Serve in tall mugs or glasses topped with whipped cream and with cinnamon sticks to stir.

scant 3 cups milk

1 cup espresso or very strong coffee

3 tablespoons vanilla sugar, plus extra to taste

4 ounces bittersweet chocolate, grated

Frothy Hot Chocolate

Real hot chocolate doesn't come as a powder in a packet—it is made with the best chocolate you can afford, whisked in hot milk until really frothy. This recipe uses bittersweet chocolate, but for a special treat you could use Mexican chocolate, which is flavored with almonds, cinnamon, and vanilla, and sweetened with sugar. All the ingredients are crushed together in a special mortar, and heated over coals. The powdered mixture is then shaped into discs, which can be bought in specialty stores.

SERVES FOUR

1 Pour the milk into a pan. Split the vanilla bean lengthways using a sharp knife to reveal the seeds, and add it to the pan of milk; the vanilla seeds and the bean will flavor the milk.

2 Add the chocolate. The amount to use depends on personal taste—start with a smaller amount if you are unsure of the flavor, and taste at the beginning of step 3, adding more if necessary.

3 Heat the chocolate milk gently, stirring until all the chocolate has melted and the mixture is smooth, then whisk with a wire whisk or a molinollo until the mixture boils. Remove the vanilla bean from the pan and divide the drink among four mugs or heatproof glasses. Serve the hot chocolate immediately.

4 cups milk

1 vanilla bean

2–4 ounces bittersweet chocolate, grated

Appetizers
and Snacks

THE PERFECT APPETIZER OR SNACK TO SERVE WITH DRINKS
SHOULD LOOK FANTASTIC, TASTE DELICIOUS AND REQUIRE
THE MINIMUM OF EFFORT TO PREPARE. THE RECIPES IN THIS
CHAPTER DO JUST THAT, BRINGING TOGETHER DELICIOUS
COMBINATIONS OF FLAVORS, TEXTURES, AROMAS AND
COLORS TO WHET THE PALATE BEFORE THE MAIN COURSE.

Hummus

This classic Middle Eastern garbanzo dip is flavored with garlic and sesame seed paste.
A little ground cumin can also be added, and olive oil can be stirred in to enrich the hummus, if you like.
It is delicious served with wedges of toasted pita bread or crudités.

SERVES FOUR TO SIX

1 Using a potato masher or fork, coarsely mash the garbanzo beans in a bowl. If you like a smoother purée, process the garbanzos in a food processor or blender until a smooth paste is formed.

2 Mix the sesame seed paste into the bowl of garbanzos, then stir in the chopped garlic cloves and lemon juice. Season to taste with freshly ground black pepper and salt, and if needed, add a little water. Serve the hummus at room temperature.

14-ounce can garbanzo beans, drained

4 tablespoons sesame seed paste

2 garlic cloves, chopped

juice of ½–1 lemon

EXTRAS *Process 2 roasted red bell peppers with the garbanzo beans, then continue as above. Serve sprinkled with lightly toasted pine nuts and paprika mixed with olive oil.*

Baba Ghanoush

Adjust the amount of eggplant, garlic, and lemon juice in this richly flavored Middle Eastern dip, depending on how creamy, garlicky, or sharp you want it to be. The dip can served with a garnish of chopped fresh cilantro leaves, olives, or pickled cucumbers. Hot pepper sauce or a little ground coriander can be added, too.

SERVES TWO TO FOUR

1 large or 2 medium eggplant

2–4 garlic cloves, chopped

6–10 tablespoons sesame seed paste

juice of 1 lemon, or to taste

1 Place the eggplant directly over a flame or on the coals of a barbecue. Turn the eggplant fairly frequently until deflated and the skin is evenly charred. Remove from the heat with tongs. Alternatively, place under a hot broiler, turning frequently, until charred.

2 Put the eggplant in a plastic bag and seal the top tightly, or place in a bowl, and cover with crumpled paper towels. Let cool for 30–60 minutes.

3 Peel off the blackened skin from the eggplant, reserving the juices. Chop the eggplant flesh, either by hand for a coarse texture or in a food processor for a smooth purée. Put the eggplant in a bowl and stir in the reserved juices.

4 Add the garlic and sesame seed paste to the eggplant and stir until smooth. Stir in the lemon juice. If the mixture becomes too thick, add 1–2 tablespoons water. Season with salt and ground black pepper to taste and spoon into a serving bowl. Serve at room temperature.

Mushroom Caviar

The name caviar refers to the dark color and texture of this dish of chopped mushrooms. Serve the mushroom mixture in individual serving dishes with toasted rye bread rubbed with cut garlic cloves, to accompany. Chopped hard-cooked egg, scallion, and parsley, the traditional garnishes for caviar, can be added as a garnish.

SERVES FOUR

1 Heat the oil in a large pan, add the mushrooms, shallots, and garlic, and cook, stirring occasionally, until browned. Season with salt, then continue cooking until the mushrooms give up their moisture.

2 Continue cooking, stirring frequently, until the moisture has evaporated and the mushrooms are brown and dry.

3 Put the mixture in a food processor or blender and process briefly until a chunky paste is formed. Spoon the mushroom caviar into dishes and serve.

3 tablespoons olive or vegetable oil

1 pound mushrooms, coarsely chopped

5–10 shallots, chopped

4 garlic cloves, chopped

EXTRAS *For a rich wild mushroom caviar, soak ¼–½ ounce dried porcini in about ½ cup water for about 30 minutes. Add the porcini and their soaking liquid to the browned mushrooms in step 2 and cook for about 1 minute longer. Continue as in the recipe. Serve with wedges of lemon, for their tangy juice.*

Brandade of Salt Cod

There are many versions of this creamy French salt cod purée: some contain mashed potatoes, others truffles. Serve the brandade with warmed crispbread or crusty bread for a really tasty appetizer, or for a light lunch serve the brandade and bread with a tomato and basil salad. You can omit the garlic from the brandade, if you like, and serve toasted slices of French bread rubbed with garlic instead.

SERVES SIX

7 ounces salt cod

1 cup extra virgin olive oil

4 garlic cloves, crushed

1 cup heavy or whipping cream

1 Soak the fish in cold water for 24 hours, changing the water frequently. Drain the fish well. Cut the fish into pieces, place in a shallow pan, and pour in enough cold water to cover. Heat the water until it is simmering and poach the fish for 8 minutes, until it is just cooked. Drain the fish, then remove the skin and bones.

2 Combine the extra virgin olive oil and crushed garlic cloves in a small pan and heat gently. In another pan, heat the heavy cream until it just starts to simmer.

3 Put the cod into a food processor, process it briefly, then gradually add alternate amounts of the garlic-flavored olive oil and cream, while continuing to process the mixture. The aim is to create a purée with the consistency of mashed potato.

4 Season to taste with freshly ground black pepper, then scoop the brandade into a serving bowl or onto individual serving plates, and serve with crispbread or crusty bread.

Chopped Egg and Scallions

This dish is one of the oldest dishes in Jewish culinary history. It is delicious served sprinkled with chopped parsley and onion rings on crackers, piled on toast, or used as a sandwich or bagel filling. Serve chopped egg and onion as part of a buffet with a selection of dips and toppings.

SERVES FOUR TO SIX

1 Put the eggs in a large pan and cover with cold water. Bring the water to a boil and when it boils, reduce the heat, and simmer over low heat for 10 minutes.

2 Hold the cooked eggs under cold running water (if too hot to handle, place the eggs in a strainer and hold under the running water). When cool, remove the shells from the eggs, and discard. Dry the eggs and chop coarsely.

3 Place the chopped eggs in a large bowl, add the onions, season generously with salt and black pepper, and mix well. Add enough mayonnaise or chicken fat to bind the mixture together. Stir in the mustard, if using, and chill before serving.

8–10 eggs

6–8 scallions and/or 1 yellow or white onion, very finely chopped, plus extra to garnish

4–6 tablespoons mayonnaise or rendered chicken fat

mild French whole-grain mustard, to taste (optional if using mayonnaise)

COOK'S TIP *The amount of rendered chicken fat or mayonnaise required will depend on how much onion you use in this dish.*

Israeli Cheese with Green Olives

In Israel, mild white cheeses spiked with seasonings, such as this one that is flavored with piquant green olives, are served with drinks and little crackers or toast. It is also very good served for brunch—spread generously on chunks of fresh, crusty bread or bagels.

SERVES FOUR

6–7 ounces farmer's cheese

2½ ounces feta cheese, preferably sheep's milk, lightly crumbled

20–30 pitted green olives, some chopped, the rest halved or cut into fourths

2–3 large pinches of fresh thyme, plus extra to garnish

1 Place the soft white cheese in a mixing bowl and stir with the back of a spoon or a fork until soft and smooth. Add the crumbled feta cheese and stir the two cheeses together until they are thoroughly combined.

2 Add all the olives and the pinches of fresh thyme to the cheese mixture and mix thoroughly.

3 Spoon the mixture into a bowl, sprinkle with thyme, and serve with crackers, toast, chunks of bread or bagels.

Yogurt Cheese in Olive Oil

In Greece, sheep's yogurt is hung in cheesecloth to drain off the whey before being patted into balls of soft cheese. Here, the cheese is bottled in extra virgin olive oil with dried chiles and fresh herbs to make a wonderful gourmet gift or aromatic appetizer. It is delicious spread on thick slices of toast as a snack or a light lunch.

FILLS TWO 1-POUND JARS

1 Sterilize a 12-inch square of cheesecloth by soaking it in boiling water. Drain and lay it over a large plate. Season the yogurt generously with salt and tip onto the center of the cheesecloth. Bring up the sides of the cheesecloth and tie firmly with string.

2 Hang the bag on a pantry door handle or other suitable position where it can be suspended over a bowl to catch the whey. Leave for 2–3 days, until the yogurt stops dripping.

3 Sterilize two 1-pound glass Mason jars or jelly jars by heating them in the oven at 300°F for 15 minutes.

4 Mix the crushed dried chiles and herbs. Take teaspoonfuls of the cheese and roll into balls with your hands. Lower into the jars, sprinkling each layer with the herb mixture.

5 Pour the oil over the cheese until completely covered. Store in the refrigerator for up to 3 weeks. To serve, spoon the cheese out of the jars with a little of the flavored olive oil and spread on slices of lightly toasted bread.

4 cups sheep's strained plain yogurt

2 teaspoons crushed dried chiles or chili powder

2 tablespoons chopped fresh herbs, such as rosemary, and thyme or oregano

about 1¼ cups extra virgin olive oil, preferably garlic-flavored

Eggs Mimosa

Mimosa describes the fine yellow and white grated egg in this dish, which looks very similar to the flower of the same name. The eggs taste delicious when garnished with black pepper and basil leaves. Grated egg yolk can also be used as a garnish for a variety of other savory dishes, such as sauces, soups, and rice dishes.

MAKES TWENTY

1 Reserve two of the hard-cooked eggs and halve the remainder. Carefully remove the yolks with a teaspoon and blend them with the avocados, garlic, and oil, adding freshly ground black pepper and salt to taste. Spoon or pipe the mixture into the halved egg whites using a pastry bag with a ½-inch or star nozzle.

2 Sift the remaining egg whites and sprinkle over the filled eggs. Sift the yolks and arrange on top. Arrange the filled egg halves on a serving platter.

12 eggs, hard-cooked and peeled

2 ripe avocados, halved and pitted

1 garlic clove, crushed

1 tablespoon olive oil

COOK'S TIP

You can prepare the mimosa garnish in advance and keep it in the refrigerator. Do not combine the egg white and yolk at this stage, but store in separate, airtight containers.

Bacon-rolled Enokitake Mushrooms

The Japanese name for this dish is *Obimaki enoki*: an *obi* (belt or sash) is made from bacon and wrapped around enokitake mushrooms before they are broiled. The strong, smoky flavor of the bacon complements the subtle flavor of mushrooms. Small heaps of ground white pepper can be offered with these savories, if you like.

1 pound fresh enokitake mushrooms

6 rindless smoked fatty bacon strips

4 lemon wedges

SERVES FOUR

1 Cut off the root part of each enokitake cluster ¾ inch from the end. Do not separate the stems. Cut the bacon strips in half lengthwise.

2 Divide the enokitake into 12 equal bunches. Take one bunch, then place the middle of the enokitake near the edge of one bacon strip, with 1–1½ inches of enokitake protruding at each end.

3 Carefully roll up the bunch of enokitake in the bacon. Tuck any straying short stems into the bacon and slide the bacon slightly upward at each roll to cover about 1½ inches of the enokitake. Secure the end of the bacon roll with a toothpick. Repeat using the remaining enokitake and bacon to make 11 more rolls.

4 Preheat the broiler to high. Place the enokitake rolls on an oiled wire rack. Broil both sides until the bacon is crisp and the enokitake start to char. This takes 10–13 minutes.

5 Remove the enokitake rolls and place on a board. Using a fork and knife, chop each roll in half in the middle of the bacon belt. Arrange the top part of the enokitake roll standing upright, the bottom part lying down next to it. Add a wedge of lemon to each portion and serve.

Walnut and Goat Cheese Bruschetta

The combination of toasted walnuts and melting goat cheese is lovely in this simple appetizer, served with a pile of salad greens. Toasting the walnuts helps to enhance their flavor. Walnut bread is readily available in most large supermarkets and makes an interesting alternative to ordinary crusty bread, although this can be used if walnut bread is unavailable.

SERVES FOUR

1 Preheat the broiler. Lightly toast the walnut pieces, then remove, and set aside. Put the walnut bread on a foil-lined broiler rack and toast on one side. Turn the slices over and drizzle each with 1 tablespoon of the French dressing.

2 Cut the goat cheese into twelve slices and place three on each piece of bread. Broil for about 3 minutes, until the cheese is melting and beginning to brown.

3 Transfer the bruschetta to serving plates, sprinkle with the toasted walnuts, and drizzle with the remaining French dressing. Serve the bruschetta immediately with salad greens.

½ cup walnut pieces

4 thick slices walnut bread

½ cup French dressing

200g/7 ounces chèvre or other semi-soft goat cheese

COOK'S TIP *Use walnut bread slices from a slender loaf, so that the portions are not too wide. If you can buy only a large loaf, cut the slices in half to make neat, chunky pieces.*

Baked Eggs with Creamy Leeks

This simple but elegant appetizer is perfect for last-minute entertaining or quick dining. Garnish the baked eggs with crisp, fried fresh sage leaves and serve with warm, fresh crusty bread for a special meal. Small- to medium-size leeks (less than 1 inch in diameter) are best for this dish, as they have the most tender flavor and only require a short cooking time.

SERVES FOUR

1 Preheat the oven to 375°F. Generously butter the base and sides of four ramekins.

2 Melt the butter in a skillet and cook the leeks over medium heat, stirring frequently, for 3–5 minutes, until softened and translucent, but not browned.

3 Add 3 tablespoons of the cream and cook over low heat for 5 minutes, until the leeks are very soft and the cream has thickened a little. Season to taste.

4 Place the ramekins in a small roasting pan and divide the leeks among them. Break an egg into each, spoon over the remaining cream, and season.

5 Pour boiling water into the roasting pan to come about halfway up the sides of the ramekins. Transfer the pan to the oven and bake in the preheated oven for about 10 minutes, until just set. Serve piping hot.

1 tablespoon butter, plus extra for greasing

8 ounces small leeks, thinly sliced

5–6 tablespoons whipping cream

4 medium–large eggs

COOK'S TIP *For a slightly different result, beat the eggs with the remaining whipping cream and seasoning in step 4 and spoon over the leeks, then bake in the roasting pan as for step 5.*

Red Onion and Olive Pissaladière

For a taste of the Mediterranean, try this French-style pizza—it makes a delicious and easy snack. Cook the sliced red onions slowly until they are caramelized and sweet before piling them into the pastry shells. To prepare the recipe in advance, pile the cooled onions onto the pastry round and chill the pissaladière until you are ready to bake it.

SERVES SIX

1 Preheat the oven to 425°F. Heat the oil in a large, heavy skillet and cook the onions gently, stirring frequently, for 15–20 minutes, until they are soft and golden. Season to taste.

2 Roll out the dough thinly on a floured surface. Cut out a 13-inch round and transfer it to a lightly dampened cookie sheet.

3 Spread the onions over the dough in an even layer to within ½ inch of the edge. Sprinkle the olives on top. Bake the tart for 20–25 minutes, until the pastry is risen and deep golden. Cut into wedges and serve warm.

5 tablespoons extra virgin olive oil

1¼ pounds small red onions, thinly sliced

1¼ pounds puff pastry dough, thawed if frozen

¾ cup small pitted black olives

Figs with Prosciutto and Roquefort

Fresh figs are a delicious treat, whether you choose dark purple, yellowy green, or green-skinned varieties. When they are ripe, you can split them open with your fingers to reveal the soft, sweet flesh full of edible seeds. In this easy, stylish dish, figs and honey balance the richness of the ham and cheese. Serve with warm bread for a simple appetizer before any rich main course.

SERVES FOUR

1 Preheat the broiler. Cut the figs into fourths and place on a foil-lined broiler rack. Tear each slice of prosciutto into two or three pieces and crumple them up on the foil beside the figs. Brush the figs with 1 tablespoon of the honey and cook under the broiler until lightly browned.

2 Crumble the Roquefort cheese and divide among four plates, setting it to one side. Add the honey-grilled figs and ham and pour over any cooking juices caught on the foil. Drizzle the remaining honey over the figs, ham, and cheese, and serve seasoned with plenty of freshly ground black pepper.

8 fresh figs

3 ounces prosciutto

3 tablespoons honey

**3 ounces
Roquefort cheese**

Crisp Fried Whitebait

This must be one of the simplest of all classic fish dishes and it is absolutely delicious with lemon wedges and thinly sliced brown bread and butter. If you like, serve the whitebait with a simple lemon and herb dip—mix ⅔ cup plain yogurt with the rind of one lemon and 3 tablespoons chopped fresh herbs. Serve chilled.

SERVES FOUR

oil, for deep-frying

⅔ cup milk

1 cup all-purpose flour

1 pound whitebait

COOK'S TIP *Most whitebait are sold frozen. Thaw them before use and dry them thoroughly on paper towels before flouring.*

1 Heat the oil in a large pan or deep-fryer. Put the milk in a shallow bowl and spoon the flour into a paper bag. Season the flour well with salt and pepper.

2 Dip a handful of the whitebait into the bowl of milk, drain them well, then pop them into the paper bag. Shake gently to coat them evenly in the seasoned flour, then transfer to a plate. Repeat until all the fish have been coated. This is the easiest method of flouring whitebait before frying, but don't add too many at once to the bag, or they will stick together.

3 Heat the oil for deep-frying to 375°F or until a cube of stale bread, dropped into the oil, browns in about 20 seconds. Add a batch of whitebait, preferably in a frying basket, and deep-fry for 2–3 minutes, until crisp and golden brown. Drain and keep hot while you cook the rest. Serve very hot.

Soups

SOUP IS ONE OF THE MOST VERSATILE DISHES AROUND AND

CAN BE SERVED AS AN ELEGANT APPETIZER OR A WARMING

MEAL. FROM CHILLED SUMMER SOUPS TO WARMING

WINTER BROTHS, THEY ARE INCREDIBLY EASY TO MAKE AND

ONLY NEED A FEW INGREDIENTS AND FLAVORINGS TO

CREATE FABULOUS, MOUTHWATERING RESULTS.

Avocado Soup

This delicious soup has a fresh, delicate flavor and a wonderful color. For added zest, add a generous squeeze of lime juice or spoon 1 tablepoon salsa into the soup just before serving. Choose ripe avocados for this soup—they should feel soft when gently pressed. Keep very firm avocados at room temperature for 3–4 days, until they soften. To speed ripening, place in a brown paper bag.

SERVES FOUR

1 Cut the avocados in half, remove the peel, and lift out the pits. Chop the flesh coarsely and place it in a food processor with 3–4 tablespoons of the sour cream. Process until smooth.

2 Heat the chicken stock in a pan. When it is hot, but still below simmering point, stir in the rest of the cream with salt to taste.

3 Gradually stir the avocado mixture into the hot stock. Heat gently but do not let the mixture approach boiling point.

4 Chop the cilantro. Ladle the soup into individual heated bowls and sprinkle each portion with chopped cilantro and black pepper. Serve immediately.

2 large ripe avocados

1¼ cups sour cream

4 cups well-flavored chicken stock

small bunch of fresh cilantro

Vichyssoise

This classic, chilled summer soup of leeks and potatoes was first created in the 1920s by Louis Diat, chef at the New York Ritz-Carlton. He named it after Vichy near his home in France. The soup can be sharpened with lemon juice, enriched with swirls of cream and garnished with chives.

SERVES FOUR TO SIX

¼ cup sweet butter

1 pound 5 ounces leeks, white parts only, thinly sliced

9 ounces mealy potatoes (such as King Edward or Maris Piper), peeled and cut into chunks

6 cups half and half light chicken stock or water and milk

1 Melt the sweet butter in a heavy pan and cook the leeks, covered, for 15–20 minutes, until they are soft but not browned.

2 Add the potato chunks and cook over low heat, uncovered, for a few minutes.

3 Stir in the stock or water and milk, with salt and pepper to taste. Bring to a boil, then reduce the heat, and partly cover the pan. Simmer for 15 minutes, or until the potatoes are soft.

4 Cool, then process the soup until smooth in a blender or food processor. Strain the soup into a bowl. Taste and adjust the seasoning and add a little ice water if it seems too thick.

5 Chill the soup for at least 4 hours, or until very cold. Taste the chilled soup for seasoning again before serving. Pour the soup into bowls and serve.

EXTRAS
To make a fabulous chilled leek and sorrel or watercress soup, add about 1 cup shredded sorrel to the soup at the end of cooking. Finish and chill as in the main recipe, then serve the soup garnished with a little pile of finely shredded sorrel. The same quantity of watercress can also be used.

Avgolemono

The name of this popular Greek soup means egg and lemon, the two essential ingredients that produce a light, nourishing soup. The soup also contains orzo, which is Greek, rice-shaped pasta, but you can use any small shape. Serve the soup with thin slices of lightly toasted bread and add a garnish of very thin lemon slices for a pretty appearance on special occasions.

SERVES FOUR TO SIX

1 Pour the chicken stock into a large pan and bring to a boil. Add the orzo pasta or other small pasta shapes and cook for 5 minutes, or according to the packet instructions.

2 Beat the eggs until they are frothy, then add the lemon juice and a tablespoon of cold water. Slowly stir in a ladleful of the hot chicken stock, then add one or two more. Remove the pan from the heat, then pour in the egg mixture, and stir well. Season to taste with salt and freshly ground black pepper and serve immediately. (Do not let the soup boil once the egg, lemon juice, and stock mixture has been added, or it will curdle.)

7½ cups chicken stock

½ cup orzo pasta

3 eggs

juice of 1 large lemon

Simple Cream of Onion Soup

This wonderfully soothing soup has a deep, buttery flavor that is achieved with only a few ingredients and the minimum of fuss. It makes delicious comfort food on a cold day. Use homemade stock if you have it, or buy fresh stock for the best flavor. Crisp croûtons or chopped chives complement the smooth soup when sprinkled over just before serving.

SERVES FOUR

½ cup sweet butter

2¼ pounds yellow onions, sliced

4 cups good chicken or vegetable stock

⅔ cup heavy cream

1 Melt 6 tablespoons of the sweet butter in a large, heavy pan. Set about 7 ounces of the onions aside and add the rest to the pan. Stir to coat in the butter, then cover, and cook very gently for about 30 minutes. The onions should be very soft and tender, but not browned.

2 Add the stock, 1 teaspoon salt, and freshly ground black pepper to taste. Bring to a boil, reduce the heat, and simmer for 5 minutes, then remove from the heat.

3 Let the soup cool, then process it in a blender or food processor. Return the soup to the rinsed pan.

4 Meanwhile, melt the remaining butter in another pan and cook the remaining onions over low heat, covered, until soft but not browned. Uncover and continue to cook the onions gently until they turn golden yellow.

5 Add the cream to the soup and reheat it gently until hot, but do not let it boil. Taste and adjust the seasoning. Add the buttery onions and stir for 1–2 minutes, then ladle the soup into bowls. Serve the soup immediately.

COOK'S TIP *Adding the second batch of onions gives texture and a lovely buttery flavor to this soup. Make sure the onions do not brown or crisp.*

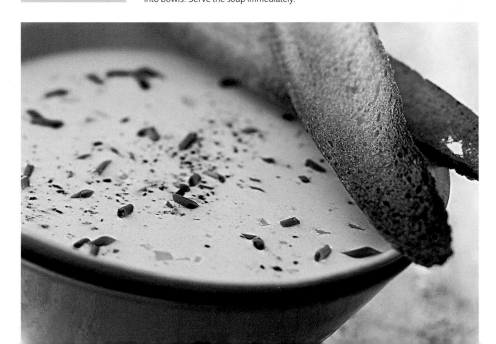

Cappelletti in Broth

This soup is traditionally served in northern Italy on Santo Stefano (St Stephen's Day, the day after Christmas) and on New Year's Day as a welcome light change from all the special celebration food. Cappelletti are little stuffed pasta resembling hats in shape.

SERVES FOUR

5 cups chicken stock

1 cup fresh or dried cappelletti

about 3 tablespoons finely chopped fresh flat leaf parsley (optional)

about 2 tablespoons freshly grated Parmesan cheese

1 Pour the chicken stock into a large pan and bring to a boil. Add a little seasoning to taste, then drop in the pasta.

2 Stir well and bring back to a boil. Lower the heat to a simmer and cook according to the instructions on the packet, until the pasta is *al dente*, that is, tender but still firm to the bite.

3 Swirl in the finely chopped fresh flat leaf parsley, if using, then taste and adjust the seasoning, if necessary. Ladle into four warmed soup plates, then sprinkle with the freshly grated Parmesan cheese, and serve immediately.

COOK'S TIP *If you don't have homemade stock, use two 11-ounce cans of condensed beef consommé, adding water as instructed, or chilled commercial stock.*

Tiny Pasta in Broth

This Italian soup is ideal for a light supper served with ciabatta bread and also makes a delicious first course for an *al fresco* supper. A wide variety of different types of *pastina* or soup pasta are available, including stellette (stars), anellini (tiny thin rounds), risoni (rice-shaped), and farfalline (little butterflies). Choose just one shape or a combination of different varieties for an interesting result.

SERVES FOUR

5 cups beef stock

¾ cup dried tiny soup pasta

2 pieces bottled roasted red bell pepper, about 2 ounces

coarsely shaved Parmesan cheese

1 Bring the beef stock to a boil in a large pan. Add seasoning to taste, then drop in the dried soup pasta. Stir well and bring the stock back to a boil.

2 Reduce the heat so that the soup simmers and cook for 7–8 minutes, or according to the packet instructions, until the pasta is *al dente*, that is, tender but still firm to the bite.

3 Drain the pieces of roasted bell pepper and dice them finely. Place them in the base of four warmed soup plates. Taste the soup for seasoning before ladling it into the soup plates. Serve immediately, topped with shavings of Parmesan.

Potato and Roasted Garlic Broth

Roasted garlic takes on a mellow, sweet flavor that is subtle, not overpowering, in this delicious vegetarian soup. Choose mealy potatoes for this soup, such as Maris Piper, Estima, Cara, or King Edward—they will give the soup a delicious velvety texture. Serve the broth piping hot with melted Cheddar or Swiss cheese on French bread, as the perfect winter warmer.

SERVES FOUR

1 Preheat the oven to 375°F. Place the unpeeled garlic bulbs or bulb in a small roasting pan and bake for 30 minutes, until soft in the center.

2 Meanwhile, parboil the potatoes in a large pan of lightly salted boiling water for 10 minutes.

3 Simmer the stock in another pan for 5 minutes. Drain the potatoes and add them to the stock.

4 Squeeze the garlic pulp into the soup, reserving a few whole cloves, stir, and season to taste. Simmer for 15 minutes and serve topped with whole garlic cloves and parsley.

2 small or 1 large whole head of garlic (about 20 cloves)

4 medium potatoes (about 1¼ pounds in total), diced

7½ cups good-quality vegetable stock

chopped flat leaf parsley, to garnish

Winter Squash Soup with Tomato Salsa

Creamy butternut squash makes good soup with very few additional ingredients. Select a really good bought salsa for this soup and add a sprinkling of chopped fresh oregano or marjoram as a garnish.

SERVES FOUR TO FIVE

1 large butternut squash or small pumpkin, halved and seeded

5 tablespoons garlic-flavored olive oil

2 onions, chopped

4–8 tablespoons tomato salsa

1 Preheat the oven to 425°F. Place the butternut squash or pumpkin on a cookie sheet, brush with some of the oil, and roast for 25 minutes. Reduce the temperature to 375°F and cook for 20–25 minutes more, or until the squash is tender.

2 Heat the remaining oil in a large, heavy pan and cook the chopped onions over low heat for about 10 minutes, or until softened.

3 Meanwhile, scoop the squash out of its skin, adding it to the pan. Pour in 5 cups water and stir in 1 teaspoon salt and plenty of black pepper. Bring to a boil, cover, and simmer gently for 10 minutes.

4 Cool the soup slightly, then process it in a blender or food processor to a smooth purée. Alternatively, press the soup through a fine strainer with the back of a spoon. Reheat without boiling, then ladle it into warmed bowls. Top each serving with a spoonful of salsa and serve.

Lima Bean, Sun-dried Tomato, and Pesto Soup

This soup is so quick and easy to make: The key is to use a good-quality homemade or bought fresh stock for the best result. Using plenty of pesto and sun-dried tomato paste gives the soup a rich flavor, rather like minestrone. As an alternative to lima beans, navy or cannellini beans will make good substitutes.

SERVES FOUR

1 Put the stock in a pan with the lima beans and bring just to a boil. Reduce the heat and stir in the tomato paste and pesto. Cook gently for 5 minutes.

2 Transfer six ladlefuls of the soup to a blender or food processor, scooping up plenty of the beans. Process until smooth, then return the purée to the pan.

3 Heat gently, stirring frequently, for 5 minutes, then season if necessary. Ladle into four warmed soup bowls and serve with warm crusty bread or breadsticks.

3¾ cups chicken or vegetable stock

2 x 14-ounce cans lima beans, drained and rinsed

4 tablespoons sun-dried tomato paste

5 tablespoons pesto

Stilton and Watercress Soup

A good creamy Stilton and plenty of peppery watercress bring maximum flavor to this rich, smooth soup, which is superlative in small portions. Arugula can be used as an alternative to watercress—both leaves are an excellent source of iron. When choosing any salad greens, look for crisp, fresh leaves and reject any wilted or discolored greens.

SERVES FOUR TO SIX

1 Pour the stock into a pan and bring almost to a boil. Remove and discard any very large stalks from the watercress. Add the watercress to the pan and simmer gently for 2–3 minutes, until tender.

2 Crumble the cheese into the pan and simmer for 1 minute more, until the cheese has started to melt. Process the soup in a blender or food processor, in batches if necessary, until very smooth. Return the soup to the pan.

3 Stir in the cream and check the seasoning. The soup will probably not need any extra salt, as the blue cheese is already quite salty. Heat the soup gently, without boiling, then ladle it into warm bowls.

2½ cups chicken or vegetable stock

8 ounces watercress

5 ounces Stilton or other blue cheese

⅔ cup light cream

Fish and Shellfish

THE DELICATE TASTE OF FISH AND SHELLFISH IS PERFECTLY
SUITED TO SUBTLE, SIMPLE FLAVORINGS SUCH AS FRESH
HERBS, CITRUS JUICE, SUCCULENT TOMATOES OR SMOKY
BACON. THE FABULOUS RECIPES IN THIS CHAPTER MAKE
THE MOST OF SIMPLE, SEASONAL INGREDIENTS TO ACHIEVE
TRULY WONDERFUL DISHES.

Sea Bass in a Salt Crust

Baking fish in a crust of sea salt seals in and enhances its flavor. Any firm fish can be cooked in this way. Decorate with a garnish of seaweed or blanched samphire and lemon slices, and break open the crust at the table to release the glorious aroma. Serve the fish with baby new potatoes roasted with olive oil and a sprinkling of dried rosemary, and steamed green vegetables, such as broccoli or green beans.

SERVES FOUR

1 Preheat the oven to 475°F. Fill the cavity of the fish with the sprigs of fresh fennel, rosemary, and thyme, and grind over some of the mixed peppercorns.

2 Spread half the salt on a shallow cookie sheet (ideally oval) and lay the sea bass on it. Cover the fish all over with a ½-inch layer of salt, pressing it down firmly. Moisten the salt lightly by spraying with water from an atomizer. Bake the fish for 30–40 minutes, until the salt crust is just beginning to color.

3 Bring the sea bass to the table in its salt crust. Use a sharp knife to break open the crust and cut into four portions.

1 sea bass, about 2¼ pounds, cleaned and scaled

1 sprig each of fresh fennel, rosemary, and thyme

mixed peppercorns

4½ pounds coarse sea salt

Roast Cod Wrapped in Prosciutto with Vine Tomatoes

Wrapping chunky fillets of cod in wafer-thin slices of prosciutto keeps the fish succulent and moist, at the same time adding flavor and visual impact. Serve with baby new potatoes and an herb salad for a stylish supper or lunch dish.

SERVES FOUR

1 Preheat the oven to 425°F. Pat the fish thoroughly dry on paper towels and remove any stray bones. Season lightly on both sides with salt and pepper.

2 Place one fillet in an ovenproof dish and drizzle 1 tablespoon of the oil over it. Cover with the second fillet, laying the thick end on top of the thin end of the lower fillet to create an even shape. Lay the prosciutto over the fish, overlapping the slices to cover the fish in an even layer. Tuck the ends of the prosciutto under the fish and tie it in place at intervals with fine string.

3 Using kitchen scissors, snip the tomato vines into four portions and add to the dish. Drizzle the tomatoes and prosciutto with the remaining oil and season lightly. Roast for about 35 minutes, until the tomatoes are tender and lightly colored and the fish is cooked through. Test the fish by piercing one end of the parcel with the tip of a sharp knife to check that it flakes easily.

4 Slice the fish and transfer the portions to warm plates, adding the tomatoes. Spoon over the cooking juices from the dish and serve immediately.

2 thick skinless cod fillets, each weighing about 13 ounces

5 tablespoons extra virgin olive oil

3 ounces prosciutto, thinly sliced

14 ounces tomatoes, on the vine

Tonno con Piselli

This Jewish Italian dish of fresh tuna and peas is especially enjoyed at Passover, which falls in spring. Before the days of the freezer, little peas were eaten only at this time of year when they were in season. At other times of the year garbanzos were used instead—they give a heartier result.

SERVES FOUR

12 ounces tuna steaks

2½ cups fresh tomato sauce

3 cups fresh shelled or frozen peas

3 tablespoons chopped fresh flat leaf parsley

1 Preheat the oven to 375°F. Sprinkle the tuna steaks on each side with salt and plenty of freshly ground black pepper and place in a shallow ovenproof dish, in a single layer.

2 Bring the tomato sauce to a boil, then add the fresh shelled or frozen peas and chopped fresh flat leaf parsley. Pour the sauce and peas evenly over the fish steaks in the ovenproof dish and bake in the preheated oven, uncovered, for about 20 minutes, or until the fish is tender. Serve the fish, sauce, and peas immediately, straight from the dish.

VARIATION *This recipe works well with other types and cuts of fish. Use tuna fillets in place of the steaks or try different fish steaks, such as salmon or swordfish.*

Phyllo-wrapped Fish

Select a chunky variety of tomato sauce for this simple but delicious recipe. The choice of fish can be varied according to what is in season and what is freshest on the day of purchase. When working with phyllo pastry, keep it covered with plastic wrap or a damp dishtowel, as once it's exposed to air, it dries out quickly and is difficult to handle.

SERVES THREE TO FOUR

about 4½ ounces phyllo pastry (6–8 large sheets)

about 2 tablespoons olive oil, for brushing

1 pound salmon or cod steaks or fillets

2½ cups fresh tomato sauce

1 Preheat the oven to 400°F. Take a sheet of phyllo pastry, brush with a little olive oil, and cover with a second sheet of pastry. Place a piece of fish on top of the pastry, toward the bottom edge, then top with 1–2 spoonfuls of the tomato sauce, spreading it out in an even layer.

2 Roll the fish in the pastry, taking care to enclose the filling completely. Brush with a little olive oil. Arrange on a cookie sheet and repeat with the remaining fish and pastry. You should have about half the sauce remaining, to serve with the fish.

3 Bake for 10–15 minutes, or until golden. Meanwhile, reheat the remaining sauce. Serve immediately with the remaining sauce.

Poached Fish in Spicy Tomato Sauce

A selection of white fish fillets are used in this Middle-Eastern dish—cod, haddock, hake, or halibut are all good. Serve the fish with flat breads, such as pita, and a spicy tomato relish. It is also good with couscous or rice and salad greens with a refreshing lemon juice dressing.

SERVES EIGHT

1 Heat the tomato sauce with the harissa and cilantro in a large pan. Add seasoning to taste and bring to a boil.

2 Remove the pan from the heat and add the fish to the hot sauce. Return to the heat and bring the sauce to a boil again. Reduce the heat and simmer very gently for about 5 minutes, or until the fish is tender. (Test with a fork: if the flesh flakes easily, then it is cooked.)

3 Taste the sauce and adjust the seasoning, adding more harissa if necessary. Serve hot or warm.

2½ cups fresh tomato sauce

½–1 teaspoon harissa

4 tablespoons chopped fresh cilantro leaves

3¼ pounds mixed white fish fillets, cut into chunks

COOK'S TIP

Harissa is a chili paste spiced with cumin, garlic, and coriander. It is fiery and should be used with care until you are familiar with the flavor. Start by adding a small amount and then add more after tasting the sauce.

Fish with Tomato and Pine Nuts

Whole fish marinated in lemon juice and cooked with pine nuts in a spicy tomato sauce is a specialty of Jewish cookery, particularly as a festival treat for Rosh Hashanah, the Jewish New Year. The fish may be cooked and served with head and tail on, as here, or if you like, with these removed. A simple garnish of flat leaf parsley improves the appearance of this delicious dish.

SERVES SIX TO EIGHT

2¼–3¼ pounds fish, such as snapper, cleaned, with head and tail left on

juice of 2 lemons

scant ¾ cup pine nuts, toasted

1½ cups spicy tomato sauce

1 Prick the fish all over with a fork and rub with ½ teaspoon salt. Put the fish in a roasting pan or large dish and pour over the lemon juice. Let stand for 2 hours.

2 Preheat the oven to 350°F. Sprinkle half of the pine nuts over the base of an ovenproof dish, top with half of the sauce, then add the fish and its marinade. Add the remaining tomato sauce and the remaining pine nuts.

3 Cover the ovenproof dish tightly with a lid or foil and bake in the preheated oven for 30 minutes, or until the fish is tender. Serve the fish immediately, straight from the dish.

Baked Salmon with Green Sauce

When buying whole salmon, there are several points to consider—the skin should be bright and shiny, the eyes should be bright, and the tail should look fresh and moist. Baking the salmon in foil produces a moist result, rather like poaching, but with the ease of baking. Garnish the fish with thin slices of cucumber and dill to conceal any flesh that may look ragged after skinning and serve with lemon wedges.

SERVES SIX TO EIGHT

4½–6¼-pound salmon, cleaned with head and tail left on

3–5 scallions, thinly sliced

1 lemon, thinly sliced

2½ cups watercress sauce or herb mayonnaise

1 Preheat the oven to 350°F. Rinse the salmon and lay it on a large piece of foil. Stuff the fish with the sliced scallions and layer the lemon slices inside and around the fish, then sprinkle with plenty of salt and ground black pepper.

2 Loosely fold the foil around the fish and fold the edges over to seal. Bake for about 1 hour.

3 Remove the fish from the oven and let stand, still wrapped in the foil, for about 15 minutes, then unwrap the parcel and leave the fish to cool.

4 When the fish is cool, carefully lift it onto a large plate, retaining the lemon slices. Cover the fish tightly with plastic wrap and chill for several hours.

5 Before serving, discard the lemon slices from around the fish. Using a blunt knife to lift up the edge of the skin, carefully peel the skin away from the flesh, avoiding tearing the flesh, and pull out any fins at the same time.

6 Chill the watercress sauce or herb mayonnaise before serving. Transfer the fish to a serving platter and serve the sauce separately.

VARIATION

Instead of cooking a whole fish, prepare 6–8 salmon steaks. Place each fish steak on an individual square of foil, then top with a slice of onion and a slice of lemon, and season generously with salt and ground black pepper. Loosely wrap the foil up around the fish, fold the edges to seal, and place the parcels on a cookie sheet. Bake the steaks for 10–15 minutes, or until the flesh is opaque. Serve the fish cold with the chilled watercress sauce or herb mayonnaise.

Haddock with Fennel Butter

Fresh fish tastes fabulous cooked in a simple herb butter. Here the licorice flavor of fennel complements the haddock beautifully to make a simple dish ideal for a dinner party. If you can buy only small haddock fillets, fold them in half before baking, or use cod as an alternative. Serve tiny new potatoes and an herb salad with the fish to make a light, summery main course.

SERVES FOUR

1 Preheat the oven to 425°F. Season the fish on both sides with salt and pepper. Melt one-fourth of the butter in a skillet, preferably nonstick, and cook the fish fillets over medium heat briefly on both sides.

2 Transfer the fish to a shallow ovenproof dish. Cut four wafer-thin slices from the lemon and squeeze the juice from the remainder over the fish. Place the lemon slices on top and then bake for 15–20 minutes, or until the fish is cooked.

3 Meanwhile, melt the remaining butter in the skillet and add the fennel and a little seasoning.

4 Transfer the cooked fish to plates and pour the cooking juices into the herb butter. Heat gently for a few seconds, then pour the herb butter over the fish. Serve immediately.

1½ pounds haddock fillet, skinned and cut into 4 portions

¼ cup butter

1 lemon

3 tablespoons coarsely chopped fennel

Crab and Cucumber Wraps

This dish is a modern twist on the ever-popular Chinese classic, crispy Peking duck with pancakes. In this quick-and-easy version, crisp, refreshing cucumber and full-flavored dressed crab are delicious with spicy-sweet hoi-sin sauce in warm tortilla wraps. Serve the wraps as an appetizer for four people, or as a main course for two.

SERVES TWO

1 Cut the cucumber into small even-size batons. Scoop the dressed crab into a small mixing bowl, add a little freshly ground black pepper, and mix lightly to combine.

2 Heat the tortillas gently, one at a time, in a heavy skillet until they begin to color on each side.

3 Spread a tortilla with 2 tablespoons hoi-sin sauce, then sprinkle with one-fourth of the cucumber. Arrange one-fourth of the seasoned crab meat down the center of each tortilla and roll up. Repeat with the remaining ingredients. Serve immediately.

½ **cucumber**

1 **medium dressed crab**

4 **small wheat tortillas**

8 **tablespoons hoi-sin sauce**

Scallops with Fennel and Bacon

This dish is a delicious combination of succulent scallops and crispy bacon, served on a bed of tender fennel and melting mascarpone. If you can't get large scallops (known as king scallops), buy the smaller queen scallops and serve a dozen per person. If you buy scallops in the shell, wash and keep the pretty fan-shaped shells to serve a range of fish dishes in.

SERVES TWO

1 Trim, halve, and slice the fennel, reserving and chopping any feathery tops. Blanch the slices in boiling water for about 3 minutes, until softened, then drain.

2 Preheat the broiler to medium. Place the fennel in a shallow flameproof dish and season with salt and pepper. Dot with the mascarpone and broil for about 5 minutes, until the cheese has melted and the fennel is lightly browned.

3 Meanwhile, pat the scallops dry on paper towels and season lightly. Cook the bacon in a large, heavy skillet, until crisp and golden, turning once. Drain and keep warm. Cook the scallops in the bacon fat for 1–2 minutes on each side, until cooked through.

4 Transfer the fennel to serving plates and crumble or snip the bacon into bitesize pieces over the top. Pile the scallops on the bacon and sprinkle with any reserved fennel tops.

2 small fennel bulbs

generous ½ cup mascarpone cheese

8 large scallops, shelled

3 ounces thin smoked fatty bacon strips

Shrimp and New Potato Stew

New potatoes with plenty of flavor, such as Jersey Royals, Maris Piper, or Nicola, are essential for this effortless stew. Use a good quality jar of tomato and chili sauce; there are now plenty available in the supermarkets. For a really easy supper dish, serve with warm, crusty bread to mop up the delicious sauce, and mixed salad greens.

SERVES FOUR

1½ pounds small new potatoes, scrubbed

½ cup fresh cilantro

12-ounce jar tomato and chili sauce

11 ounces cooked peeled shrimp, thawed and drained if frozen

1 Cook the potatoes in lightly salted, boiling water for 15 minutes, until tender. Drain and return to the pan.

2 Finely chop half the cilantro and add to the pan with the tomato and chili sauce and 6 tablespoons water. Bring to a boil, reduce the heat, cover, and simmer gently for 5 minutes.

3 Stir in the shrimp and heat briefly until they are warmed through. Do not overheat the shrimp or they will quickly shrivel, becoming tough and tasteless. Spoon into shallow bowls and serve sprinkled with the remaining cilantro, torn into pieces.

Meat and Poultry

WITH THE SIMPLE ADDITION OF A FEW WELL-CHOSEN
INGREDIENTS, MEAT AND POULTRY CAN BE TRANSFORMED
INTO EXCITING, INNOVATIVE DISHES. FROM STEAK TO DUCK
AND FROM PORK TO PHEASANT, THIS CHAPTER INCLUDES A
WONDERFUL SELECTION OF DISHES THAT ARE EQUALLY
SUITED TO A QUICK FAMILY SUPPER OR A DINNER PARTY.

Beef Patties with Onions and Peppers

This is a firm family favorite. It is easy to make and delicious, and it can be varied by adding other vegetables, such as sliced red bell peppers, broccoli, or mushrooms. The patties are very versatile and can be served in a variety of ways—with chunky homemade French fries, with crusty bread, or with rice and a ready-made tomato sauce.

SERVES FOUR

1 Place the ground beef, chopped onion, and 1 tablespoon of the garlic-flavored oil in a bowl and mix well. Season well and form into four large or eight small patties.

2 Heat the remaining oil in a large, nonstick pan, then add the patties, and cook on both sides until browned. Sprinkle over 1 tablespoon water and add a little seasoning.

3 Cover the patties with the sliced onions and bell peppers. Sprinkle in another 1 tablespoon water and a little seasoning, then cover the pan. Reduce the heat to very low and braise for 20–30 minutes.

4 When the onions are turning golden brown, remove the pan from the heat. Serve the patties with onions and bell peppers.

1¼ pounds lean ground beef

4 onions, 1 finely chopped and 3 sliced

2 tablespoons garlic-flavored olive oil or olive oil

2–3 green bell peppers, seeded and sliced lengthwise into strips

Steak with Warm Tomato Salsa

A refreshing, tangy salsa of tomatoes, scallions, and balsamic vinegar makes a colorful topping for chunky, pan-fried steaks. Choose round or sirloin—whichever is your favorite—and if you do not have a nonstick skillet, broil the steak instead for the same length of time. Serve with potato wedges and mixed salad greens with a mustard dressing.

SERVES TWO

1 Trim any excess fat from the steaks, then season on both sides with salt and pepper. Heat a nonstick skillet and cook the steaks for about 3 minutes on each side for medium rare. Cook for a little longer if you like your steak well cooked.

2 Meanwhile, put the tomatoes in a heatproof bowl, cover with boiling water, and leave for 1–2 minutes, until the skins start to split. Drain and peel the tomatoes, then halve them, and scoop out the seeds. Dice the tomato flesh. Thinly slice the scallions.

3 Transfer the steaks to plates and keep warm. Add the vegetables, balsamic vinegar, 2 tablespoons water, and a little seasoning to the cooking juices in the skillet and stir briefly until warm, scraping up any meat residue. Spoon the salsa over the steaks to serve.

**2 steaks, about
¾ inch thick**

3 large plum tomatoes

2 scallions

**2 tablespoons
balsamic vinegar**

North African Lamb

This dish is full of contrasting flavors that create a rich, spicy, and fruity main course. For best results, use lamb that still retains some fat, as this will help keep the meat moist and succulent during roasting. Serve the lamb with couscous or mixed white and wild rice, sprinkled with chopped cilantro. Roasted chunks of red and yellow bell peppers, eggplant, and zucchini, tossed in olive oil and cooked in the oven with the lamb, complete the meal.

SERVES FOUR

1 Preheat the oven to 400°F. Season the lamb with salt and pepper. Heat a skillet, preferably nonstick, and cook the lamb on all sides until beginning to brown. Transfer to a roasting pan, reserving any fat in the skillet.

2 Peel the onions and cut each into six wedges. Toss with the lamb and roast for about 30-40 minutes, until the lamb is cooked through and the onions are deep golden brown.

3 Tip the lamb and onions back into the skillet. Mix the harissa with 1 cup boiling water and add to the roasting pan. Scrape up any residue in the pan and pour the mixture over the lamb and onions. Stir in the prunes and heat until just simmering. Cover and simmer for 5 minutes, then serve.

1½ pounds lamb tenderloin or shoulder steaks, cut into chunky pieces

5 small onions

1½ teaspoons harissa

½ cup ready-to-eat pitted prunes, halved

Lamb Steaks with Red Currant Glaze

This classic, simple dish is absolutely delicious and is an excellent, quick recipe for cooking on the barbecue. The tangy flavor of red currants is a traditional accompaniment to lamb. It is good served with new potatoes and fresh peas tossed in butter.

SERVES FOUR

1 Reserve the tips of the rosemary and finely chop the remaining leaves. Rub the chopped rosemary, salt, and pepper all over the lamb.

2 Preheat the broiler. Heat the red currant jelly gently in a small pan with 2 tablespoons water and a little seasoning. Stir in the vinegar.

3 Place the lamb steaks on a foil-lined broiler rack and brush with a little of the red currant glaze. Cook under the broiler for about 5 minutes on each side, until deep golden, brushing frequently with more red currant glaze.

4 Transfer the lamb to warmed plates. Tip any juices from the foil into the remaining glaze and heat through gently. Pour the glaze over the lamb and serve, garnished with the reserved rosemary sprigs.

4 large fresh rosemary sprigs

4 lamb leg steaks

5 tablespoons red currant jelly

2 tablespoons raspberry or red wine vinegar

Paprika Pork

This chunky, goulash-style dish is rich with bell peppers and paprika. Broiling the bell peppers before adding them to the meat really brings out their sweet, vibrant flavor. Rice or buttered boiled potatoes go particularly well with the rich pork.

SERVES FOUR

2 red, 1 yellow, and 1 green bell peppers, seeded

1¼ pounds lean pork tenderloin

3 tablespoons paprika

11-ounce jar or tub of tomato sauce with herbs or garlic

1 Preheat the broiler. Cut the bell peppers into thick strips and sprinkle in a single layer on a foil-lined broiler rack. Broil for 20–25 minutes, until the edges of the strips are lightly charred.

2 Meanwhile, cut the pork into chunks. Season with salt and pepper and cook in a nonstick skillet for about 5 minutes, until beginning to brown.

3 Transfer the meat to a heavy pan and add the paprika, tomato sauce, 1¼ cups water, and a little seasoning. Bring to a boil, reduce the heat, cover, and simmer gently for 30 minutes.

4 Add the broiled bell peppers and cook for 10–15 minutes more, until the meat is tender. Taste for seasoning and serve immediately.

Pork Kabobs

The word kabob comes from Arabic and means on a skewer. Use pork tenderloin for these kabobs because it is lean and tender, and cooks very quickly. They are good served with rice, or stuffed into warmed pita bread with some shredded lettuce leaves.

SERVES FOUR

1¼ pounds lean pork tenderloin

8 large, thick scallions, trimmed

½ cup barbecue sauce

1 lemon

1 Cut the pork into 1-inch cubes. Cut the scallions into 1-inch long sticks.

2 Preheat the broiler to high. Oil the wire rack and spread out the pork cubes on it. Broil the pork until the juices drip, then dip the pieces in the barbecue sauce, and put back on the broiler. Broil for 30 seconds on each side, repeating the dipping process twice more. Set aside and keep warm.

3 Gently broil the scallions until soft and slightly brown outside. Do not dip in the barbecue sauce. Thread about four pieces of pork and three scallion pieces onto each of eight bamboo skewers.

4 Arrange the skewers on a platter. Cut the lemon into wedges and squeeze a little lemon juice over each skewer. Serve immediately, offering the remaining lemon wedges separately.

COOK'S TIP

If you are cooking the pork on a barbecue, soak the skewers overnight in water to prevent them from burning. Keep the skewer handles away from the fire and turn them frequently.

Drunken Chicken

In this traditional Chinese dish, cooked chicken is marinated in sherry, fresh ginger root, and scallions for several days. Because of the lengthy preparation time, it is important to use a very fresh bird from a reputable supplier. Fresh herbs can be added as an additional garnish, if you like.

SERVES FOUR TO SIX

1 chicken, about 3 pounds

½-inch piece of fresh ginger root, thinly sliced

2 scallions, trimmed, plus extra to garnish

1¼ cups dry sherry

1 Rinse and dry the chicken inside and out. Place the ginger and scallions in the body cavity. Put the chicken in a large pan or flameproof casserole and just cover with water. Bring to a boil, skim off any scum, and cook for 15 minutes.

2 Turn off the heat, cover the pan or casserole tightly, and leave the chicken in the cooking liquid for 3–4 hours, by which time it will be cooked. Drain well, reserving the stock. Pour 1¼ cups of the stock into a pitcher.

3 Remove the skin and cut the chicken into neat pieces. Divide each leg into a drumstick and thigh. Make two more portions from the wings and some of the breast meat. Finally, cut away the remainder of the breast pieces (still on the bone) and divide each piece into two even-size portions.

4 Arrange the chicken portions in a shallow dish. Rub salt into the chicken and cover with plastic wrap. Leave in a cool place for several hours or overnight in the refrigerator.

5 Later, lift off any fat from the stock, add the sherry, and pour over the chicken. Cover again and leave in the refrigerator to marinate for 2–3 days, turning occasionally.

6 When ready to serve, cut the chicken through the bone into chunky pieces and arrange on a large serving platter. Garnish the chicken with scallion shreds.

VARIATION
To serve as a cocktail snack, take the meat off the bones, cut it into bitesize pieces, then spear each piece on a toothpick to serve.

Soy-marinated Chicken

Two simple flavors, soy sauce and orange, combine to make this mouthwatering dish. Serving the chicken on a bed of asparagus turns the dish into a special treat. Wilted spinach or shredded greens work well as an everyday alternative. Boiled egg noodles or steamed white rice make a good accompaniment.

SERVES FOUR

4 skinless, boneless chicken breast portions

1 large orange

2 tablespoons dark soy sauce

14 ounces medium asparagus spears

1 Slash each chicken portion diagonally and place them in a single layer in a shallow, ovenproof dish. Halve the orange, squeeze the juice from one half, and combine it with the soy sauce. Pour this over the chicken. Cut the remaining orange into wedges and place these on the chicken. Cover and let marinate for several hours.

2 Preheat the oven to 350°F. Turn the chicken over and bake, uncovered, for 20 minutes. Turn the chicken over again and bake for 15 minutes more, or until cooked through.

3 Meanwhile, cut off any tough ends from the asparagus and place in a skillet. Pour in enough boiling water just to cover and cook gently for 3–4 minutes, until just tender. Drain and arrange on warmed plates, then top with the chicken and orange wedges. Spoon over the cooking juices and season with black pepper. Serve immediately.

Chicken Scallops with Lemon and Serrano Ham

Chicken scallops are flattened chicken breast fillets—they cook quicker than normal breast portions and absorb flavors more readily. In this light summery dish, the chicken absorbs the delicious flavors of the ham and lemon. It can be assembled in advance, so is good for entertaining.

SERVES FOUR

1 Preheat the oven to 350°F. Beat the butter with plenty of freshly ground black pepper and set aside. Place the chicken portions on a large sheet of plastic wrap, spacing them well apart. Cover with a second sheet, then beat with a rolling pin until the portions are half their original thickness.

2 Transfer the chicken to a large, shallow ovenproof dish and crumple a slice of ham on top of each. Cut eight thin slices from the lemon and place two on each slice of ham.

3 Dot with the pepper butter and bake for about 30 minutes, until the chicken is cooked. Transfer to serving plates and spoon over any juices from the dish.

3 tablespoons butter, softened

4 skinless chicken breast fillets

4 slices Serrano ham

1 lemon

Roast Chicken with Herb Cheese, Chile, and Lime Stuffing

Whether you are entertaining guests or cooking a family meal, a tasty chicken is a sure winner every time. This is a modern twist on the classic roast chicken—the stuffing is forced under the chicken skin, which helps to produce a wonderfully flavored, succulent flesh.

SERVES FIVE TO SIX

1 Preheat the oven to 400°F. Using first the point of a knife and then your fingers, separate the skin from the meat across the chicken breast and over the tops of the legs. Use the knife to loosen the first piece of skin, then carefully run your fingers underneath, taking care not to tear the skin.

2 Grate the lime and beat the rind into the cream cheese together with the chopped chile. Pack the cream cheese stuffing under the skin, using a teaspoon, until fairly evenly distributed. Push the skin back into place, then smooth your hands over it to spread the stuffing in an even layer.

3 Put the chicken in a roasting pan and squeeze the juice from the lime over the top. Roast for 1½ hours, or until the juices run clear when the thickest part of the thigh is pierced with a skewer. If necessary, cover the chicken with foil toward the end of cooking if the top starts to become too browned.

4 Carve the chicken and arrange on a warmed serving platter. Spoon the pan juices over it and serve immediately.

4-pound chicken

1 lime

½ cup cream cheese with herbs and garlic

1 mild fresh red chile, seeded and finely chopped

Turkey Patties

So much better than store-bought burgers, these light patties are delicious served hamburger-style in split and toasted buns with relish, salad greens, and chunky fries. They can also be made using chicken, lamb, pork, or beef. If you are making them for children, shape the mixture into 12 equal-sized rounds and serve in mini-rolls or in rounds stamped out from sliced bread.

SERVES SIX

1½ pounds ground turkey

1 small red onion, finely chopped

small handful of fresh thyme leaves

2 tablespoons lime-flavored olive oil

1 Combine the turkey, onion, thyme, 1 tablespoon of the oil, and seasoning. Cover and chill for up to 4 hours to let the flavors steep, then divide the mixture into six equal portions and shape into round patties.

2 Preheat a griddle pan. Brush the patties with half of the remaining lime-flavored olive oil, then place them on the pan, and cook for 10–12 minutes. Turn the patties over, brush with more oil, and cook for 10–12 minutes on the second side, or until cooked right through. Serve the patties immediately.

VARIATION

As well as using other types of ground meat, you could try chopped oregano or parsley in place of the thyme, and lemon-flavored oil instead of lime.

Guinea Fowl with Whiskey Sauce

Served with creamy, sweet mashed potato and lightly boiled whole baby leeks, guinea fowl is magnificent with a rich, creamy whiskey sauce. If you don't like the flavor of whiskey, then substitute brandy, Madeira, or Marsala. Or, to make a non-alcoholic version, use freshly squeezed orange juice instead. Garnish with fresh thyme sprigs or other fresh herbs.

SERVES FOUR

2 guinea fowl, each weighing about 2¼ pounds

6 tablespoons whiskey

⅔ cup well-flavored chicken stock

⅔ cup heavy cream

1 Preheat the oven to 400°F. Brown the guinea fowl on all sides in a roasting pan on the stovetop, then turn it breast uppermost, and transfer the pan to the oven. Roast for about 1 hour, until the guinea fowl are golden and cooked through. Transfer the guinea fowl to a warmed serving dish, cover with foil, and keep warm.

2 Pour off the excess fat from the pan, then heat the juices on the stovetop, and stir in the whiskey. Bring to a boil and cook until reduced. Add the stock and cream and simmer again until reduced slightly. Strain and season to taste.

3 Carve the guinea fowl and serve on individual plates, arranged around the chosen vegetable accompaniments. Sprinkle with plenty of freshly ground black pepper. Spoon a little of the sauce over each portion and serve the rest separately.

Pheasant Cooked in Port with Mushrooms

This warming dish is delicious served with mashed root vegetables and shredded cabbage or leeks. Marinating the pheasant in port helps to moisten and tenderize the meat, which can often be slightly dry. If you prefer, marinate the pheasant in a full-bodied red wine and use white mushrooms.

2 pheasants, cut into portions

1¼ cups port

¼ cup butter

10 ounces chestnut mushrooms, halved if large

SERVES FOUR

1 Place the pheasant in a bowl and pour over the port. Cover and marinate for 3–4 hours or overnight, turning the portions occasionally.

2 Drain the meat thoroughly, reserving the marinade. Pat the portions dry on paper towels and season lightly with salt and pepper. Melt three-fourths of the butter in a skillet and cook the pheasant portions on all sides for about 5 minutes, until deep golden. Drain well, transfer to a plate, then cook the mushrooms in the fat remaining in the skillet for 3 minutes.

3 Return the pheasant to the pan and pour in the reserved marinade with scant 1 cup water. Bring to a boil, reduce the heat, and cover, then simmer gently for about 45 minutes, until the pheasant is tender and cooked through.

4 Using a slotted spoon, carefully remove the pheasant portions and mushrooms from the skillet and keep warm. Bring the cooking juices to a boil and boil vigorously for 3–5 minutes, until they are reduced and slightly thickened. Strain the juices through a fine strainer and return them to the skillet. Whisk in the remaining butter over gentle heat until it has melted, season to taste, then pour the juices over the pheasant and mushrooms, and serve.

Duck with Plum Sauce

Sharp plums cut the rich flavor of duck wonderfully well in this updated version of an old English dish. Duck is often considered to be a fatty meat, but modern breeding methods have made leaner ducks widely available. For an easy dinner party main course, serve the duck with creamy mashed potatoes and celery root, and steamed broccoli.

SERVES FOUR

4 duck portions

1 large red onion, finely chopped

1¼ pounds ripe plums, pitted and cut into fourths

2 tablespoons red currant jelly

1 Prick the duck skin all over with a fork to release the fat during cooking and help give a crisp result, then place the portions in a heavy skillet, skin side down.

2 Cook the duck pieces for 10 minutes on each side, or until golden brown and cooked right through. Remove the duck from the skillet using a slotted spoon and keep warm.

3 Pour away all but 2 tablespoons of the duck fat, then stir-fry the onion for 5 minutes, or until golden. Add the plums and cook for 5 minutes, stirring frequently. Add the jelly and mix well.

4 Replace the duck portions and cook for 5 minutes more, or until thoroughly reheated. Season to taste before serving.

Vegetarian Dishes

FRESH-TASTING VEGETABLES, MILD EGGS,

RICH AND CREAMY CHEESES AND AROMATIC HERBS

AND SPICES ARE GREAT PARTNERS AND CAN BE COMBINED

TO MAKE A DELICIOUS ARRAY OF VEGETARIAN MEALS.

ENJOY WONDERFUL DISHES SUCH AS BAKED

STUFFED VEGETABLES, RICHLY FLAVORED TARTS

AND LIGHT-AS-AIR SOUFFLÉS.

Eggplant with Cheese Sauce

This wonderfully simple dish of eggplant in cheese sauce is delicious hot and the perfect dish to assemble ahead of time ready for baking at the last minute. Kashkaval cheese is particularly good in this recipe—it is a hard yellow cheese made from sheep's milk and is originally from the Balkans. Serve with lots of crusty bread to mop up the delicious eggplant-flavored cheese sauce.

SERVES FOUR TO SIX

1 Layer the eggplant slices in a bowl or colander, sprinkling each layer with salt, and let drain for at least 30 minutes. Rinse well, then pat dry with paper towels.

2 Heat the oil in a skillet, then cook the eggplant slices until golden brown on both sides. Remove from the skillet and set aside.

3 Preheat the oven to 350°F. Mix most of the grated cheese into the savory white or Béchamel sauce, reserving a little to sprinkle on top of the finished dish.

4 Arrange a layer of the eggplant in an ovenproof dish, then pour over some sauce. Repeat, ending with sauce. Sprinkle with the reserved cheese. Bake for 35–40 minutes until golden.

2 large eggplant, cut into ¼-inch thick slices

about 4 tablespoons olive oil

2½ cups savory white sauce or Béchamel sauce

3½ cups grated cheese, such as kashkaval, Swiss, or a mixture of Parmesan and Cheddar

Mushroom Stroganoff

This creamy mixed mushroom sauce is ideal for a dinner party. Serve it with toasted buckwheat, brown rice, or a mixture of wild rices. For best results, choose a variety of different mushrooms—wild mushrooms, such as chanterelles, ceps, and morels add a delicious flavor and texture to the stroganoff, as well as adding color, and producing a decorative appearance.

SERVES FOUR

2 tablespoons butter

2 pounds mixed mushrooms, cut into bitesize pieces, including ⅔ white mushrooms and ⅓ assorted wild or exotic mushrooms

1½ cups white wine sauce

1 cup sour cream

1 Melt the butter in a pan and quickly cook the mushrooms, in batches, over high heat, until brown. Transfer the mushrooms to a bowl after cooking each batch.

2 Add the sauce to the juices remaining in the pan and bring to a boil, stirring. Reduce the heat and replace the mushrooms with any juices from the bowl. Stir well and heat for a few seconds, then remove from the heat.

3 Stir the sour cream into the cooked mushroom mixture and season to taste with salt and lots of freshly ground black pepper. Heat through gently for a few seconds, if necessary, then transfer to warm plates and serve immediately.

Red Onion and Goat Cheese Pastries

These attractive little tartlets couldn't be easier to make. Garnish them with fresh thyme sprigs and serve with a selection of salad greens and a tomato and basil salad for a light lunch or quick supper. A wide variety of different types of goat cheeses is available—the creamy log-shaped types without a rind are most suitable for these pastries. Ordinary onions can be used instead of red, if you like.

SERVES FOUR

1 Heat the oil in a large, heavy skillet, add the onions, and cook over gentle heat for 10 minutes, or until softened, stirring occasionally to prevent them from browning. Add seasoning to taste and cook for 2 minutes more. Remove the skillet from the heat and let cool.

2 Preheat the oven to 425°F. Unroll the puff pastry dough and using a 6-inch plate as a guide, cut out four rounds. Place the pastry rounds on a dampened cookie sheet and, using the point of a sharp knife, score a border, ¾ inch inside the edge of each pastry round.

3 Divide the onions among the pastry rounds and top with the goat cheese. Bake for 25–30 minutes, until golden brown.

1 tablespoon olive oil

1 pound red onions, sliced

15-ounce packet ready-rolled puff pastry dough

1 cup diced goat cheese

EXTRAS *To make richer-flavored pastries and add to the variety, spread the pastry base with red or green pesto or tapenade before you top with the goat cheese and cooked onions.*

Baked Leek and Potato Gratin

Potatoes baked in a creamy cheese sauce make the ultimate comfort dish, whether served as an accompaniment to pork or fish dishes or, as here, with plenty of leeks and melted cheese as a main course. When preparing leeks, separate the leaves and rinse them thoroughly under cold running water, as soil and grit often get caught between the layers.

SERVES FOUR TO SIX

1 Preheat the oven to 350°F. Cook the potatoes in plenty of lightly salted, boiling water for 3 minutes, until slightly softened, then drain. Cut the leeks into ½-inch lengths and blanch them in boiling water for 1 minute, until softened, then drain.

2 Turn half the potatoes into a shallow, ovenproof dish and spread them out to the edge. Cover with two-thirds of the leeks, then add the remaining potatoes. Tuck the slices of cheese and the remaining leeks in among the top layer of potatoes. Season with salt and pepper and pour the cream over.

3 Bake for 1 hour, until tender and golden. Cover with foil if the top starts to overbrown before the potatoes are tender.

2 pounds medium potatoes, thinly sliced

2 large leeks, trimmed

7 ounces ripe Brie or Camembert cheese, sliced

scant 2 cups light cream

Mushroom Polenta

This simple recipe uses freshly made polenta, but for an even easier version you can substitute ready-made polenta and slice it straight into the dish, ready for baking. The cheese and mushroom topping is also delicious on toasted herb or sun-dried tomato bread as a really speedy light lunch or supper. Any combination of mushrooms will work—try a mixture of white and wild mushrooms as an alternative.

SERVES FOUR

1 Line an 11 x 7-inch shallow baking pan with baking parchment. Bring 4 cups water with 1 teaspoon salt to a boil in a large pan. Add the polenta in a steady stream, stirring constantly. Bring back to a boil, stirring, and cook for 5 minutes, until thick and smooth. Turn the polenta into the prepared pan and spread it out into an even layer. Let cool.

2 Preheat the oven to 400°F. Melt the butter in a skillet and cook the mushrooms for 3–5 minutes, until golden. Season with salt and lots of freshly ground black pepper.

3 Turn out the polenta onto a cutting board. Peel away the parchment and cut the polenta into large squares. Pile the squares into a shallow, ovenproof dish. Sprinkle with half the cheese, then pile the mushrooms on top, and pour over their buttery juices. Sprinkle with the remaining cheese and bake for about 20 minutes, until the cheese is melting and pale golden.

1½ cups quick-cook polenta

¼ cup butter

14 ounces chestnut mushrooms, sliced

1½ cups grated Swiss cheese

Tomato and Tapenade Tarts

These delicious individual tarts look and taste fantastic, in spite of the fact that they demand very little time or effort. The mascarpone cheese topping melts as it cooks to make a smooth, creamy sauce. Cherry tomatoes have a delicious sweet flavor with a low acidity, but plum cherry tomatoes or vine-ripened tomatoes are also suitable for these tarts and will give delicious results. Red pesto can be used instead of the tapenade if you like a subtler flavor.

SERVES FOUR

1 Preheat the oven to 425°F. Lightly grease a large cookie sheet and sprinkle it with water. Roll out the pastry dough on a lightly floured surface and cut out 4 x 6½-inch rounds, using a bowl or small plate as a guide.

2 Transfer the pastry rounds to the prepared cookie sheet. Using the tip of a sharp knife, mark a shallow cut ½ inch from the edge of each round to form a rim.

3 Reserve half the tapenade and spread the rest over the pastry rounds, keeping the paste inside the marked rim. Cut half the tomatoes in half. Pile all the tomatoes, whole and halved, on the pastry, again keeping them inside the rim. Season lightly.

4 Bake for 20 minutes, until the pastry is well risen and golden. Dot with the remaining tapenade. Spoon a little mascarpone on the center of the tomatoes and season with black pepper. Bake for 10 minutes more, until the mascarpone has melted to make a sauce. Serve the tarts warm.

1¼ pounds puff pastry dough, thawed if frozen

4 tablespoons black or green olive tapenade

1¼ pounds cherry tomatoes

scant ½ cup mascarpone cheese

Stuffed Baby Squash

It is worth making the most of baby squash while they are in season. Use any varieties you can find and do not worry too much about choosing vegetables of uniform size, as an assortment of different types and sizes looks attractive. The baked vegetables can easily be shared out at the table. Serve with warm sun-dried tomato bread and a ready-made spicy tomato sauce for a hearty fall supper.

SERVES FOUR

1 Preheat the oven to 375°F. Pierce the squash in several places with the tip of a knife. Bake for 30 minutes, until the squash are tender. Leave until cool enough to handle.

2 Meanwhile, cook the rice in salted, boiling water for 12 minutes, until tender, then drain. Slice a lid off the top of each squash and scoop out and discard the seeds. Scoop out and chop the flesh.

3 Heat the oil in a skillet and cook the chopped squash for 5 minutes. Reserve 4 tablespoons of the cheese, add the remainder to the skillet with the rice and a little salt. Mix well.

4 Pile the mixture into the squash shells and place in an ovenproof dish. Sprinkle with the remaining cheese and bake for 20 minutes.

4 small squash, each about 12 ounces

1 cup mixed wild and basmati rice

4 tablespoons chili and garlic oil

1¼ cups grated Swiss cheese

Roasted Bell Peppers with Halloumi and Pine Nuts

Halloumi cheese is creamy-tasting and has a firm texture and salty flavor that contrast well with the succulent sweet bell peppers. This is a good dish to assemble in advance. Halloumi is usually served cooked and lends itself well to frying or broiling. When heated the exterior hardens while the interior softens and is similar to mozzarella cheese.

SERVES FOUR

1 Preheat the oven to 425°F. Halve the red bell peppers, leaving the stalks intact, and discard the seeds. Seed and coarsely chop the orange or yellow bell peppers. Place the red bell pepper halves on a cookie sheet and fill with the chopped bell peppers. Drizzle with half the garlic or herb olive oil and bake for 25 minutes, until the edges of the bell peppers are beginning to char.

2 Dice the cheese and tuck in among the chopped bell peppers. Sprinkle with the pine nuts and drizzle with the remaining oil. Bake for 15 minutes more, until well browned. Serve warm.

4 red and 2 orange or yellow bell peppers

4 tablespoons garlic or herb olive oil

1¾ cups halloumi cheese

½ cup pine nuts

Spicy Garbanzo Samosas

A blend of crushed garbanzo beans and coriander sauce makes an interesting alternative to the more familiar meat or vegetable fillings in these little pastries. The samosas look pretty garnished with fresh cilantro leaves and thinly sliced onion and are delicious served with a simple dip made from strained plain yogurt and chopped fresh mint leaves.

MAKES EIGHTEEN

1 Preheat the oven to 425°F. Process half the garbanzo beans to a paste in a food processor. Tip the paste into a bowl and add the whole garbanzos, the hara masala or coriander sauce, and a little salt. Mix until well combined.

2 Lay a sheet of phyllo pastry on a counter and cut into three strips. Brush the strips with a little of the oil. Place a dessertspoon of the filling at one end of a strip. Turn one corner diagonally over the filling to meet the long edge. Continue folding the filling and the pastry along the length of the strip, keeping the triangular shape. Transfer to a cookie sheet and repeat with the remaining filling and pastry.

3 Brush the pastries with any remaining oil and bake for 15 minutes, until the pastry is golden. Cool slightly before serving.

2 x 14-ounce cans garbanzo beans, drained and rinsed

½ cup hara masala or coriander sauce

10 ounces phyllo pastry

4 tablespoons chili and garlic oil

Bean Curd and Bell Pepper Kabobs

A simple coating of ground, dry-roasted peanuts pressed onto cubed bean curd provides plenty of additional flavor along with the bell peppers. Use metal or bamboo skewers for the kabobs—if you use bamboo, then soak them in cold water for 30 minutes before using to prevent them from scorching during cooking. The kabobs can also be cooked on a barbecue, if you like.

SERVES FOUR

1 Pat the bean curd dry on paper towels and then cut it into small cubes. Grind the peanuts in a blender or food processor and transfer to a plate. Turn the bean curd cubes in the nuts to coat.

2 Preheat the broiler to medium. Halve and seed the bell peppers and cut them into large chunks. Thread the chunks of bell pepper onto four large skewers with the bean curd cubes and place on a foil-lined broiler rack.

3 Broil the kabobs, turning frequently, for 10–12 minutes, or until the bell peppers and peanuts are beginning to brown. Transfer the kabobs to plates and serve with the dipping sauce.

9 ounces firm bean curd

½ cup dry-roasted peanuts

2 red and 2 green bell peppers

4 tablespoons sweet chili dipping sauce

Mixed Bean and Tomato Chili

Here, mixed beans, fiery red chile, and plenty of freshly chopped cilantro are simmered in a tomato sauce to make a delicious vegetarian chili. Always a popular dish, chili can be served with a variety of accompaniments—choose from baked potatoes, boiled rice, crusty bread, or tortillas. Garnish with slices of tomato, chopped celery, or sweet bell pepper and top with plain yogurt.

SERVES FOUR

1 Pour the tomato sauce and mixed beans into a pan. Seed and thinly slice the chile, then add it to the pan. Reserve a little of the cilantro, chop the remainder, and add it to the pan.

2 Bring the mixture to a boil, reduce the heat, cover, and simmer gently for 10 minutes. Stir the mixture occasionally and add a dash of water if the sauce starts to dry out.

3 Ladle the chili into warmed individual serving bowls. garnish with the reserved cilantro, and top with a spoonful of yogurt to serve.

14-ounce jar tomato and herb sauce

2 x 14-ounce cans mixed beans, drained and rinsed

1 fresh red chile

large handful of fresh cilantro

Cheese and Tomato Soufflés

Using a ready-made cheese sauce takes the effort out of soufflé making. The key to success when making soufflés is to whisk the egg whites thoroughly to incorporate as much air as possible. During the cooking time don't open the oven door—the cold draft could cause the delicate mixture to collapse.

SERVES SIX

1 Preheat the oven to 400°F. Turn the cheese sauce into a bowl. Thinly slice the sun-dried tomatoes and add to the bowl with generous 1 cup of the Parmesan, the egg yolks, and seasoning. Stir until well combined.

2 Brush the base and sides of six scant 1-cup ramekins with the oil and then coat the insides of the dishes with half the remaining cheese, tilting them until evenly covered.

3 Whisk the egg whites in a clean bowl until stiff. Use a large metal spoon to stir a fourth of the egg whites into the sauce, then fold in the remainder. Spoon the mixture into the prepared dishes and sprinkle with the remaining Parmesan cheese. Place on a cookie sheet and bake for 15–18 minutes, until well risen and golden. Serve the soufflés as soon as you remove them from the oven.

12-ounce tub fresh cheese sauce

2 ounces sun-dried tomatoes in olive oil, drained, plus 2 teaspoons of the oil

1½ cups freshly grated Parmesan cheese

4 extra large eggs, separated

Potato and Onion Tortilla

This deep-set omelet with sliced potatoes and onions is the best-known Spanish tortilla and makes a deliciously simple meal when served with a leafy salad and crusty bread. Tortillas are often made with a variety of ingredients—chopped red or yellow bell peppers, cooked peas, corn, or grated Cheddar or Swiss cheese can all be added to the mixture in step 2, if you like.

SERVES FOUR TO SIX

1¼ pounds medium potatoes

scant ½ cup extra virgin olive oil

2 onions, thinly sliced

6 eggs

1 Thinly slice the potatoes. Heat 5 tablespoons of the oil in a skillet and cook the potatoes, turning frequently, for 10 minutes. Add the onions and seasoning, and continue to cook gently for 10 minutes more, until the vegetables are tender.

2 Meanwhile, beat the eggs in a large bowl with a little seasoning. Tip the potatoes and onions into the eggs and mix gently. Let stand for 10 minutes.

3 Wipe out the pan skillet with paper towels and heat the remaining oil in it. Pour the egg mixture into the skillet and spread it out in an even layer. Cover and cook over very gentle heat for 20 minutes, until the eggs are just set. Serve cut into wedges.

Spiced Lentils

The combination of lentils, tomatoes, and cheese is widely used in Mediterranean cookery. The tang of feta cheese complements the slightly earthy flavor of the attractive dark lentils. True Puy lentils come from the region of France, Le Puy, which has a unique climate and volcanic soil in which they thrive.

SERVES FOUR

1½ cups Puy lentils

7 ounces feta cheese

5 tablespoons sun-dried tomato paste

small handful of fresh chervil or flat leaf parsley, chopped, plus extra to garnish

1 Place the lentils in a heavy pan with 2½ cups water. Bring to a boil, reduce the heat, and cover the pan. Simmer gently for about 20 minutes, until the lentils are just tender and most of the water has been absorbed.

2 Crumble half the feta cheese into the pan. Add the sun-dried tomato paste, chopped chervil or flat leaf parsley, and a little salt and freshly ground black pepper. Heat through for 1 minute.

3 Transfer the lentil mixture and juices to warmed plates or bowls. Crumble the remaining feta cheese on top and sprinkle with the fresh herbs to garnish. Serve the lentils immediately.

Pasta and Rice Dishes

PASTA AND RICE ARE THE PERFECT STAPLES UPON WHICH
TO BASE SIMPLE, TASTY MEALS. YOU NEED ONLY A FEW
INGREDIENTS TO RUSTLE UP DELICIOUS DISHES, FROM A
SIMPLE MIDWEEK SUPPER TO MORE ELEGANT DISHES FOR
ENTERTAINING. WHETHER YOU CHOOSE A SUBSTANTIAL
BOWL OF PASTA OR A FRAGRANT RISOTTO – THE RECIPES
IN THIS CHAPTER ARE SURE TO DELIGHT.

Spaghettini with Roasted Garlic

If you have never tried roasting garlic, then this is the recipe that will convert you to its delicious mellowed sweetness. Spaghettini is very fine spaghetti, but any long thin pasta can be used in this dish—try spaghetti, linguine, tagliatelle, or capellini. This simple pasta dish is very good served with mixed salad greens dressed with lemon juice and extra virgin olive oil.

SERVES FOUR

1 Preheat the oven to 350°F. Place the garlic in an oiled roasting pan and roast it for 30 minutes.

2 Let the garlic cool, then lay it on its side and slice off the top third with a sharp knife.

3 Hold the garlic over a bowl and dig out the flesh from each clove with the point of the knife. When all the flesh has been added to the bowl, pour in the oil, and add plenty of black pepper. Mix well.

4 Cook the pasta in a pan of salted, boiling water according to the instructions on the packet. Drain the pasta and return it to the clean pan. Pour in the oil and garlic mixture and toss the pasta vigorously over medium heat until all the strands are thoroughly coated. Serve immediately, with shavings of Parmesan.

1 whole head of garlic

14 ounces fresh or dried spaghettini

½ cup extra virgin olive oil

coarsely shaved Parmesan cheese

Spaghetti with Lemon

This is the dish to make when you get home and find there's nothing to eat. If you keep spaghetti and olive oil in the pantry, and garlic and lemons in the vegetable rack, you can prepare this delicious meal in minutes. You can also add some freshly grated Parmesan cheese if you have some.

SERVES FOUR

1 Cook the pasta in a pan of salted, boiling water according to the instructions on the packet, then drain well, and return to the pan.

2 Pour the olive oil and lemon juice over the cooked pasta, sprinkle in the slivers of garlic, and add seasoning to taste. Toss the pasta over medium to high heat for 1–2 minutes. Serve immediately in four warmed bowls.

12 ounces dried spaghetti

6 tablespoons extra virgin olive oil

juice of 1 large lemon

2 garlic cloves, cut into very thin slivers

COOK'S TIP
Spaghetti is the best type of pasta for this recipe, because the olive oil and lemon juice cling to its long thin strands. If you are out of spaghetti, use another dried long pasta shape instead, such as spaghettini, linguine, or tagliatelle.

Linguine with Arugula

This fashionable first course is very quick and easy to make at home. Arugula has an excellent peppery flavor that combines beautifully with the rich, creamy tang of fresh Parmesan cheese. Fresh Parmesan keeps well in the refrigerator for up to a month—the dried variety is a very poor substitute and bears little resemblance to the real thing.

SERVES FOUR

1 Cook the pasta in a large pan of lightly salted boiling water according to the instructions on the packet, then drain thoroughly.

2 Heat about 4 tablespoons of the olive oil in the pasta pan, then add the drained pasta, followed by the arugula. Toss over medium to high heat for 1–2 minutes, or until the arugula is just wilted, then remove the pan from the heat.

3 Tip the pasta and arugula into a large, warmed bowl. Add half the freshly grated Parmesan and the remaining olive oil. Add a little salt and black pepper to taste.

4 Toss the mixture quickly to mix. Serve immediately, sprinkled with the remaining Parmesan.

12 ounces fresh or dried linguine

½ cup extra virgin olive oil

1 large bunch arugula, about 5 ounces, stalks removed, shredded or torn

1 cup freshly grated Parmesan cheese

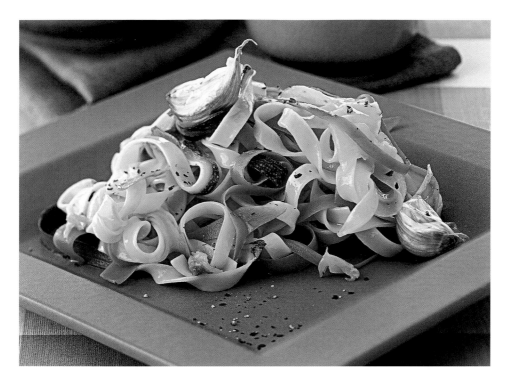

Tagliatelle with Vegetable Ribbons

Narrow strips of zucchini and carrot mingle well with tagliatelle to resemble colored pasta. Serve as a side dish, or sprinkle with freshly grated Parmesan cheese for a light appetizer or vegetarian main course. Garlic flavored olive oil is used in this dish—flavored oils, such as rosemary, chili, or basil, are widely available and are a quick way of adding flavor to pasta.

SERVES FOUR

2 large zucchini

2 large carrots

9 ounces fresh egg tagliatelle

4 tablespoons garlic flavored olive oil

1 With a vegetable peeler, cut the zucchini and carrots into long thin ribbons. Bring a large pan of salted water to a boil, then add the zucchini and carrot ribbons. Bring the water back to a boil and boil for 30 seconds, then drain, and set aside.

2 Cook the tagliatelle according to the instructions on the packet. Drain the pasta and return it to the pan. Add the vegetable ribbons, garlic flavored oil, and seasoning and toss over medium to high heat until the pasta and vegetables are glistening with oil. Serve the pasta immediately.

Spaghetti with Raw Tomato and Ricotta Sauce

This wonderfully simple uncooked sauce goes well with many different kinds of freshly cooked pasta, both long strands, such as spaghetti, tagliatelle, or linguini, and short shapes, such as macaroni, rigatoni, or penne. It is always at its best in summer when made with rich, sweet plum tomatoes that have ripened on the vine in the sun and have their fullest flavor.

SERVES FOUR

1¼ pounds ripe Italian plum tomatoes

5 tablespoons garlic-flavored olive oil

12 ounces dried spaghetti or pasta of your choice

4 ounces ricotta salata cheese, diced

1 Coarsely chop the plum tomatoes, removing the cores and as many of the seeds as you can.

2 Put the tomatoes and oil in a bowl, adding salt and pepper to taste, and stir well. Cover and leave at room temperature for 1–2 hours to let the flavors mingle.

3 Cook the spaghetti or your chosen pasta according to the packet instructions, then drain well.

4 Taste the sauce to check the seasoning before tossing it with the hot pasta. Sprinkle with the cheese and serve immediately.

Farfalle with Tuna

Bought tomato sauce and canned tuna are endlessly versatile for making weekday suppers. A variety of herbs can be added to simple pasta dishes like this one—choose from basil, marjoram, or oregano—and use fresh herbs, as the short cooking time does not allow the flavor of dried herbs to develop fully. Add a garnish of fresh oregano to this dish if you happen to have some.

SERVES FOUR

1 Cook the pasta in a large pan of lightly salted boiling water according to the instructions on the packet. Meanwhile, heat the tomato sauce in a separate pan and add the olives.

2 Drain the canned tuna and flake it with a fork. Add the tuna to the sauce with about 4 tablespoons of the water used for cooking the pasta. Taste and adjust the seasoning.

3 Drain the cooked pasta thoroughly and tip it into a large, warmed serving bowl. Pour the tuna sauce over the top and toss lightly to mix. Serve immediately.

3½ cups dried farfalle

2½ cups tomato sauce

8–10 pitted black olives, cut into rings

6-ounce can tuna in olive oil

Fettucine all'Alfredo

This simple recipe was invented by a Roman restaurateur called Alfredo, who became famous for serving it with a gold fork and spoon. Today's busy cooks will find cartons of long-life cream invaluable for this type of recipe. If you can't get fettucine, any long ribbon-like pasta can be used in this dish— try tagliatelle or slightly wider pappardelle instead.

SERVES FOUR

1 Melt the butter in a large pan. Add the cream and bring it to a boil. Simmer for 5 minutes, stirring constantly, then add the Parmesan cheese, with salt and freshly ground black pepper to taste, and turn off the heat under the pan.

2 Bring a large pan of salted water to a boil. Drop in the pasta all at once and quickly bring the water back to a boil, stirring occasionally. Cook the pasta for 2–3 minutes, or according to the instructions on the packet. Drain well.

3 Turn on the heat under the pan of cream to low, add the cooked pasta all at once, and toss until it is thoroughly coated in the sauce. Taste the sauce for seasoning. Serve immediately, with extra grated Parmesan handed around separately.

¼ cup butter

scant 1 cup heavy cream

⅔ cup freshly grated Parmesan cheese, plus extra to serve

12 ounces fresh fettucine

Pansotti with Walnut Sauce

Walnuts and cream make a rich and luscious sauce for stuffed pasta, particularly the types filled with cheese and herbs. Serve this indulgent dish with warm walnut bread and a light, fruity white wine.

SERVES FOUR

1 Put the walnuts and garlic oil in a food processor and process to a paste, adding up to ½ cup warm water through the feeder tube to slacken the consistency. Spoon the mixture into a large bowl and add the cream. Beat well to mix, then season to taste with salt and black pepper.

2 Cook the pansotti or stuffed pasta in a large pan of salted, boiling water for 4–5 minutes, or according to the instructions on the packet. Meanwhile, put the walnut sauce in a large warmed bowl and add a ladleful of the pasta cooking water to thin it.

3 Drain the pasta and tip it into the bowl of walnut sauce. Toss well, then serve immediately.

**scant 1 cup
shelled walnuts**

**4 tablespoons garlic-
flavored olive oil**

½ cup heavy cream

**12 ounces cheese and
herb-filled pansotti or
other stuffed pasta**

Rosemary Risotto with Borlotti Beans

Select a high-quality risotto in a subtle flavor as the base for this recipe. The savory beans, heady rosemary and creamy mascarpone will transform a simple product into a feast. For an even more authentic risotto flavor, replace half the water with dry white wine. Serve with a simple salad of arugula and Parmesan shavings dressed with balsamic vinegar and plenty of freshly ground black pepper.

SERVES THREE TO FOUR

14-ounce can borlotti beans

10-ounce packet vegetable or chicken risotto

4 tablespoons mascarpone cheese

1 teaspoon finely chopped fresh rosemary

1 Drain the beans, rinse under cold water, and drain again. Process about two-thirds of the beans to a fairly coarse purée in a food processor or blender. Set the remaining beans aside.

2 Make up the risotto according to the packet instructions, using the suggested quantity of water.

3 Immediately the rice is cooked, stir in the bean purée. Add the reserved beans, with the mascarpone and rosemary, then season to taste. Stir thoroughly, then cover, and let stand for about 5 minutes so that the risotto absorbs the flavors fully.

VARIATION

Fresh thyme or marjoram could be used for this risotto instead of rosemary, if you like. One of the great virtues of risotto is that it lends itself well to many variations. Experiment with plain or saffron risotto and add different herbs to make your own speciality dish.

Pancetta and Fava Bean Risotto

This moist risotto makes a satisfying, balanced meal, especially when served with cooked fresh seasonal vegetables or mixed salad greens. Add some chopped fresh herbs and Parmesan shavings as a garnish, if you like. Pancetta is dry cured pork and is the Italian equivalent of fatty bacon—either can be used in this recipe.

6 ounces smoked pancetta, diced

1¼ cups risotto rice

6¼ cups simmering herb stock

2 cups frozen baby fava beans

SERVES FOUR

1 Place the pancetta in a nonstick or heavy pan and cook gently, stirring occasionally, for about 5 minutes, until the fat runs.

2 Add the risotto rice to the pan and cook for 1 minute, stirring constantly. Add a ladleful of the simmering stock and cook, stirring constantly, until the liquid has been absorbed.

3 Continue adding the simmering stock, a ladleful at a time, until the rice is tender, and almost all the liquid has been absorbed. This will take 30–35 minutes.

4 Meanwhile, cook the fava beans in a pan of lightly salted, boiling water for about 3 minutes, until tender. Drain well and stir into the risotto. Season to taste. Spoon into a bowl and serve.

COOK'S TIP

If the fava beans are large, or if you prefer skinned beans, remove the outer skin after cooking them.

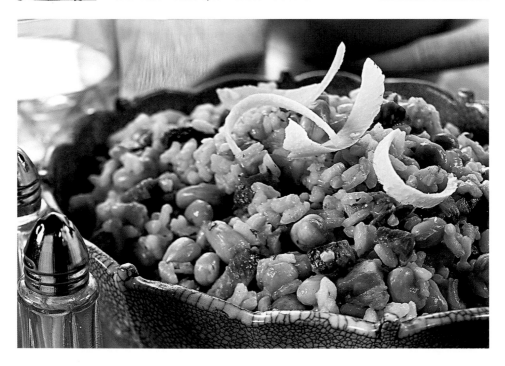

Mussel Risotto

The addition of freshly cooked mussels, aromatic cilantro, and a little cream to a packet of instant risotto can turn a simple meal into a decadent treat. Serve with a side salad for a splendid supper. Other types of cooked shellfish, such as clams or shrimp, can be used instead of mussels.

SERVES THREE TO FOUR

2 pounds fresh mussels

10-ounce packet risotto

2 tablespoons chopped fresh cilantro

2 tablespoons heavy cream

1 Scrub the mussels, discarding any that do not close when sharply tapped. Place in a large pan. Add ½ cup water and seasoning, then bring to a boil. Cover the pan and cook the mussels, shaking the pan occasionally, for 4–5 minutes, until they have opened. Drain, reserving the liquid and discarding any that have not opened. Shell most of the mussels, reserving a few in their shells for garnish. Strain the mussel liquid.

2 Make up the packet risotto according to the instructions, using the cooking liquid from the mussels and making it up to the required volume with water.

3 When the risotto is about three-fourths cooked, add the mussels to the pan. Add the cilantro and re-cover the pan without stirring in these ingredients.

4 Remove the risotto from the heat, stir in the cream, cover, and let rest for a few minutes. Spoon into a warmed serving dish, garnish with the reserved mussels in their shells, and serve.

COOK'S TIP *For a super-quick mussel risotto, use cooked mussels in their shells—the type sold vacuum packed ready to reheat. Just reheat them according to the packet instructions and add to the made risotto with the cilantro and cream in step 3.*

Crab Risotto

This simple risotto has a subtle flavor that makes the most of delicate crab. It makes a tempting main course or appetizer. It is important to use a good quality risotto rice, which will give a deliciously creamy result, but the cooked grains are still firm to the bite.

SERVES THREE TO FOUR

2 large cooked crabs

1½ cups risotto rice

5 cups simmering fish stock

2 tablespoons mixed finely chopped fresh herbs, such as chives, tarragon, and parsley

1 One at a time, hold the crabs firmly and hit the underside with the heel of your hand. This should loosen the shell from the body. Using your thumbs, push against the body and pull away from the shell. Remove and discard the intestines and the gray gills.

2 Break off the claws and legs, then use a hammer or crackers to break them open. Using a pick, remove the meat from the claws and legs. Place the meat on a plate.

3 Using a skewer, pick out the white meat from the body cavities and place with the claw and leg meat, reserving a little white meat to garnish. Scoop out the brown meat from the shell and add to the rest of the crab meat.

4 Place the rice in a pan and add one-fourth of the stock. Bring to a boil and cook, stirring, until the liquid has been absorbed. Adding a ladleful of stock at a time, cook, stirring, until about two-thirds of the stock has been absorbed. Stir in the crab meat and herbs, and continue cooking, adding the remaining stock.

5 When the rice is almost cooked but still has some bite, remove it from the heat and adjust the seasoning. Cover and let stand for 3 minutes. Serve garnished with the reserved white crab meat.

Vegetables and Side Dishes

A FEW CAREFULLY-CHOSEN INGREDIENTS CAN BE BROUGHT

TOGETHER TO CREATE MOUTHWATERING SIDE DISHES

AND ACCOMPANIMENTS THAT WILL COMPLEMENT AND

ENHANCE ANY MAIN DISH. THIS COLLECTION OF TASTY

AND COLOURFUL COMBINATIONS OF VEGETABLES MAKE

HEALTHY EATING A TEMPTING TREAT.

Japanese-style Spinach with Toasted Sesame Seeds

This Japanese speciality, known as *O-hitashi*, has been served as a side dish on dining tables in Japan for centuries. Seasonal green vegetables are simply blanched and cooled and formed into little towers. With a little help from soy sauce and sesame seeds, they reveal their true flavor. Serve the spinach towers with simply cooked chicken or fish, such as salmon or tuna.

SERVES FOUR

1 Blanch the spinach leaves in lightly salted boiling water for 15 seconds. For Japanese-type spinach, hold the leafy part and slip the stems into the pan. After 15 seconds, drop in the leaves and cook for 20 seconds.

2 Drain immediately and place the spinach under running water. Squeeze out all the excess water by hand. Now what looked like a large amount of spinach has become a ball, about the size of an orange. Mix the shoyu and water, then pour onto the spinach. Mix well and let cool.

3 Meanwhile, put the sesame seeds in a dry skillet and stir or toss until they start to pop. Remove from the heat and let cool.

4 Drain the spinach and squeeze out the excess sauce with your hands. Form the spinach into a log shape of about 1½ inches in diameter on a cutting board. Squeeze again to make it firm. With a sharp knife, cut it across into four cylinders.

5 Place the spinach cylinders on a large plate or individual dishes. Sprinkle with the toasted sesame seeds and a little salt and serve.

1 pound fresh young spinach

2 tablespoons shoyu

2 tablespoons water

1 tablespoon sesame seeds

COOK'S TIP *Japanese spinach, the long-leaf type with the stalks and pink root intact, is best, but you can use ordinary young spinach leaves, or any soft and deep-colored salad greens—such as watercress, arugula, or corn salad.*

Braised Lettuce and Peas with Scallions

This light vegetable dish is based on the classic French method of braising peas with lettuce and scallions in butter, and is delicious served with simply broiled fish or roast or broiled duck. A sprinkling of chopped fresh mint makes a fresh, flavorsome, and extremely pretty garnish. Other legumes such as fava beans, sugar snaps, and snow peas, can be used instead of peas to create a delicious variation.

SERVES FOUR

¼ cup butter

4 Bibb lettuces, halved lengthwise

2 bunches of scallions, trimmed

3½ cups shelled peas (about 2¼ pounds in pods)

1 Melt half the butter in a wide, heavy pan over low heat. Add the lettuces and scallions.

2 Turn the vegetables in the butter, then sprinkle in salt and plenty of freshly ground black pepper. Cover and cook the vegetables very gently for 5 minutes, stirring once.

3 Add the peas and turn them in the buttery juices. Pour in ½ cup water, then cover, and cook over gentle heat for 5 minutes more. Uncover the pan and increase the heat to reduce the liquid to a few tablespoons.

4 Stir in the remaining butter and adjust the seasoning. Transfer to a warmed serving dish and serve immediately.

EXTRAS

• Braise 9 ounces baby carrots with the lettuce.

• Cook ⅔ cup chopped smoked bacon or pancetta in the butter. Use only one bunch of scallions and stir in some finely chopped fresh parsley.

Asparagus with Lemon Sauce

Sometimes less is more: here, a simple egg and lemon dressing brings out the best in asparagus. Serve the asparagus as an appetizer or side dish; alternatively, enjoy it for a light supper, with bread and butter to mop up the juices. When buying asparagus, look for bright colored, firm spears with tight buds—avoid those with tough, woody stems. Choose even-size spears for uniform cooking.

SERVES FOUR

1 Cook the bundle of asparagus in a tall pan of lightly salted, boiling water for 7–10 minutes.

2 Drain well and arrange the asparagus in a serving dish. Reserve scant 1 cup of the cooking liquid.

3 Blend the cornstarch with the cooled, reserved cooking liquid and place in a small pan. Bring to a boil, stirring constantly, and cook over gentle heat until the sauce thickens slightly. Remove the pan from the heat and let cool slightly.

4 Beat the egg yolks thoroughly with the lemon juice and gradually stir into the cooled sauce. Cook over very low heat, stirring constantly, until the sauce is fairly thick. Be careful not to overheat the sauce or it may curdle. As soon as the sauce has thickened, remove the pan from the heat and continue stirring for 1 minute. Taste and season with salt. Let the sauce cool slightly.

5 Stir the cooled lemon sauce, then pour a little over the cooked asparagus. Cover and chill in the refrigerator for at least 2 hours before serving with the rest of the sauce to accompany.

1½ pounds asparagus, tough ends removed, and tied in a bundle

1 tablespoon cornstarch

2 egg yolks

juice of 1½ lemons

COOK'S TIP
If you like a slightly less tangy sauce, then add a little superfine sugar with the salt in step 4.

Caramelized Shallots

Sweet, golden shallots are good with all sorts of main dishes, including poultry or meat. Shallots have a less distinctive aroma than common onions and a milder flavor; they are also considered to be easier to digest. These caramelized shallots are also excellent with braised or roasted chestnuts, carrots, or chunks of butternut squash. You may like to garnish the shallots with sprigs of fresh thyme before serving.

SERVES FOUR TO SIX

1 Heat the butter or oil in a large skillet and add the shallots or onions in a single layer. Cook gently, turning occasionally, until they are lightly browned.

2 Sprinkle the sugar over the shallots and cook gently, turning the shallots in the juices, until the sugar begins to caramelize. Add the wine or port and let the mixture bubble for 4–5 minutes.

3 Add ⅔ cup water and seasoning. Cover and cook for 5 minutes, then remove the lid, and cook until the liquid evaporates and the shallots are tender and glazed. Taste and adjust the seasoning before serving.

¼ cup butter or 4 tablespoons olive oil

1¼ pounds shallots or small onions, peeled with root ends intact

1 tablespoon golden superfine sugar

2 tablespoons red or white wine or port

Cauliflower with Garlic Crumbs

This simple dish makes a great accompaniment to any meat or fish dish. When buying cauliflower, look for creamy white colored flowerets with the inner green leaves curled around the flower. Discard cauliflowers with discolored patches or yellow leaves. As an alternative, try using broccoli flowerets instead of the cauliflower. Broccoli should have a fresh appearance: avoid yellowing specimens and those that feel soft or are wilting.

SERVES FOUR TO SIX

1 Steam or boil the cauliflower in salted water until just tender. Drain and let cool.

2 Heat 4–5 tablespoons of the olive or vegetable oil in a pan, add the bread crumbs, and cook over medium heat, tossing and turning, until browned and crisp. Add the garlic, turn once or twice, then remove from the pan, and set aside.

3 Heat the remaining oil in the pan, then add the cauliflower, mashing and breaking it up a little as it lightly browns in the oil. (Do not overcook but just cook until lightly browned.)

4 Add the garlic bread crumbs to the pan and cook, stirring, until well combined, with some of the cauliflower still holding its shape. Season and serve hot or warm.

1 large cauliflower, cut into bitesize flowerets

6–8 tablespoons olive or vegetable oil

2¼ cups dry white or whole-wheat bread crumbs

3–5 garlic cloves, thinly sliced or chopped

COOK'S TIP *Serve this wonderful, garlicky cauliflower dish as they do in Italy, with cooked pasta, such as spaghetti or rigatoni.*

Summer Squash and Baby New Potatoes in Warm Dill Sour Cream

Fresh vegetables and fragrant dill are delicious tossed in a simple sour cream or yogurt sauce. Choose small squash with bright skins that are free from blemishes and bruises. To make a simpler potato salad, pour the dill sour cream over warm cooked potatoes. Serve either version of the potato salad with poached salmon or charbroiled chicken.

SERVES FOUR

1 Cut the squash into pieces about the same size as the potatoes. Put the potatoes in a pan and add water to cover and a pinch of salt. Bring to a boil, then simmer for about 10 minutes, until almost tender. Add the squash and continue to cook until the vegetables are just tender, then drain.

2 Return the vegetables to the pan and gently stir in the finely chopped fresh dill and chives.

3 Remove the pan from the heat and stir in the sour cream or yogurt. Return to the heat and heat gently until warm. Season and serve.

14 ounces mixed squash, such as yellow and green zucchini, and pale green patty pan

14 ounces tiny, baby new potatoes

1 large handful mixed fresh dill and chives, finely chopped

1¼ cups sour cream or strained plain yogurt

Baked Winter Squash with Tomatoes

Acorn, butternut, or Hubbard squash can all be used in this simple recipe. Serve the squash as a light main course, with warm crusty bread, or as a side dish for broiled meat or poultry. Canned chopped tomatoes with herbs are used in this recipe. A variety of flavored canned tomatoes is now available including garlic, onion, and olive—they are ideal for adding a combination of flavors when time is short.

SERVES FOUR TO SIX

1 Preheat the oven to 325°F. Heat the oil in a pan and cook the pumpkin or squash slices, in batches, until golden brown, removing them from the pan as they are cooked.

2 Add the tomatoes and cook over medium-high heat until the mixture is of a sauce consistency. Stir in the rosemary and season to taste with salt and pepper.

3 Layer the pumpkin slices and tomatoes in an ovenproof dish, ending with a layer of tomatoes. Bake for 35 minutes, or until the top is lightly glazed and beginning to turn golden brown, and the pumpkin is tender. Serve immediately.

3 tablespoons garlic-flavored olive oil

2¼ pounds pumpkin or orange winter squash, peeled and sliced

2 x 14-ounce cans chopped tomatoes with herbs

2–3 fresh rosemary sprigs, stems removed and leaves chopped

Stewed Okra with Tomatoes and Cilantro

This is a favorite Middle-Eastern way to prepare okra. Add wedges of lemon as a garnish so that their juice can be squeezed over the vegetables to taste. Okra, also known as lady's fingers, are narrow green lantern-shaped pods. They contain a row of seeds that ooze a viscous liquid when cooked. This liquid acts as a natural thickener in a variety of curries and soups.

SERVES FOUR TO SIX

1 Heat the tomatoes and the cinnamon, cumin, and cloves with half the cilantro in a pan, then season to taste with salt and freshly ground black pepper, and bring to a boil.

2 Add the okra and cook, stirring constantly, for 1–2 minutes. Reduce the heat to low, then simmer, stirring occasionally, for 20–30 minutes, until the okra is tender.

3 Taste for spicing and seasoning, and adjust if necessary, adding more of any one spice, salt, or pepper to taste. Stir in the remaining cilantro. Serve hot, warm, or cold.

14-ounce can chopped tomatoes with onions and garlic

generous pinch each of ground cinnamon, cumin, and cloves

6 tablespoons chopped fresh cilantro leaves

1¾ pounds okra

Tomato and Eggplant Gratin

This colorful, Mediterranean dish makes the perfect partner to broiled, pan-fried, or baked meat or poultry. If you prefer, thinly sliced zucchini can be used in this dish instead of the eggplant. Broil the zucchini for 10–15 minutes. Choose plum tomatoes if you can—they have fewer seeds than most round tomatoes, so are less watery and are ideal for cooking.

SERVES FOUR TO SIX

1 Preheat the broiler. Thinly slice the eggplant and arrange them in a single layer on a foil-lined broiler rack. Brush the eggplant slices with some of the olive oil and broil for 15–20 minutes, turning once, until golden on both sides. Brush the second side with more olive oil after turning the slices.

2 Preheat the oven to 400°F. Toss the eggplant and tomato slices together in a bowl with a little seasoning, then pile them into a shallow, ovenproof dish. Drizzle with any remaining olive oil and sprinkle with the grated Parmesan cheese. Bake for 20 minutes, until the cheese is golden and the vegetables are hot. Serve the gratin immediately.

2 medium eggplant, about 1¼ pounds

6 tablespoons olive oil

14 ounces ripe tomatoes, sliced

½ cup freshly grated Parmesan cheese

Deep-fried Artichokes

This is an Italian speciality, named *carciofi alla giudia*. The artichokes are baked, then pressed to open them, and plunged into hot oil, where their leaves twist and brown, turning the artichokes into crispy flowers. Serve with lamb or pork steaks.

SERVES FOUR

2–3 lemons, halved

4–8 small young globe artichokes

olive or vegetable oil, for deep-frying

1 Fill a large bowl with cold water and stir in the juice of one or two of the lemons. Trim and discard the stems of the artichokes, then trim off their tough ends, and remove all the tough outer leaves until you reach the pale pointed center. Carefully open the leaves of one of the artichokes by pressing it against the table or poking them open. Trim the tops if they are sharp.

2 If there is any choke inside the artichoke, remove it with a melon baller or small pointed spoon. Put the artichoke in the acidulated water and prepare the remaining artichokes in the same way.

3 Put the artichokes in a large pan and pour over water to cover. Bring to a boil, reduce the heat, and simmer for 10–15 minutes, or until partly cooked. If they are small, cook them for only 10 minutes. Drain the artichokes and leave upside down until cool enough to handle. Press them open gently, being careful not to break them apart.

4 Fill a pan with oil to a depth of 2–3 inches and heat. Add one or two artichokes at a time, with the leaves uppermost, and press down with a spoon to open up the leaves. Fry for 5–8 minutes, turning, until golden and crisp. Remove from the pan and drain on paper towels. Serve immediately, with the remaining lemon cut into wedges.

COOK'S TIP *Select immature artichokes, before their chokes have formed. If you like, you can prepare and boil them ahead and deep-fry just before serving.*

133

Leek Fritters

These crispy fried morsels are best served at room temperature, with a good squeeze of lemon juice and a sprinkling of salt and freshly grated nutmeg. Matzo meal, a traditional Jewish ingredient, is used in these fritters: it is made from crumbled matzo, an unleavened bread, similar to water biscuits. Matzo meal is used in a similar way to bread crumbs, which can also be used to make these fritters.

SERVES FOUR

1 Cook the leeks in salted, boiling water for 5 minutes, or until just tender and bright green. Drain well and let cool.

2 Chop the leeks coarsely. Put in a bowl and combine with the matzo meal, eggs, and seasoning.

3 Heat ¼ inch oil in a skillet. Using two tablespoons, carefully spoon the leek mixture into the hot oil. Cook over medium-high heat until golden brown on the underside, then turn and cook the second side. Drain on paper towels. Add more oil if needed and heat before cooking more mixture.

4 large leeks, total weight about 2¼ pounds, thickly sliced

½–¾ cup coarse matzo meal

2 eggs, lightly beaten

olive or vegetable oil, for shallow frying

Bubble and Squeak

Whether you have leftovers or cook this old-fashioned classic from fresh, be sure to give it a really good "squeak" in the pan so it turns a rich honey brown. Serve as an accompaniment to broiled pork chops or fried eggs, or simply serve with warm bread for a quick supper. If you like, cook the bubble and squeak in individual-sized portions—divide into four and form into patties before cooking.

SERVES FOUR

1 Heat 2 tablespoons of the bacon fat or oil in a heavy skillet. Add the onion and cook over medium heat, stirring frequently, until softened but not browned.

2 In a large bowl, combine the potatoes and cooked cabbage or sprouts and season with salt and plenty of pepper to taste.

3 Add the vegetables to the skillet with the cooked onions, stir well, then press the vegetable mixture into a large, even cake.

4 Cook over medium heat for about 15 minutes, until the cake is browned underneath.

5 Invert a large plate over the skillet, and, holding it tightly against the skillet, turn them both over together. Lift off the skillet, return it to the heat, and add the remaining bacon fat or oil. When hot, slide the cake back into the skillet, browned side uppermost.

6 Cook over medium heat for 10 minutes, or until the underside is golden brown. Serve hot, in wedges.

4 tablespoons bacon fat or vegetable oil

1 medium onion, finely chopped

1 pound mealy potatoes, cooked and mashed

8 ounces cooked cabbage or Brussels sprouts, finely chopped

EXTRAS *When made with vegetables from a roast dinner, the mixture can be moistened with leftover gravy, making it bubble as it cooks and giving a really delicious savory flavor.*

Fennel, Potato, and Garlic Mash

This flavorsome mash of potato, fennel, and garlic goes well with practically all main dishes, whether fish, poultry, or meat. Mealy varieties of potato, such as Pentland Squire, King Edward, or Marfona are best for mashing as they produce a light fluffy result. Waxy potatoes are more suitable for baking, or for salads, as they produce a dense, rather starchy mash.

SERVES FOUR

1 Boil the potatoes in salted water for 20 minutes, until tender.

2 Meanwhile, trim and coarsely chop the fennel, reserving any feathery tops. Chop the tops and set them aside. Heat 2 tablespoons of the oil in a heavy pan. Add the fennel, cover, and cook over low heat for 20–30 minutes, until soft but not browned.

3 Drain and mash the potatoes. Purée the fennel in a food mill or blender and beat it into the potato with the remaining oil.

4 Warm the milk or cream and beat sufficient into the potato and fennel to make a creamy, light mixture. Season to taste and reheat gently, then beat in any chopped fennel tops. Serve immediately.

1¾ pounds potatoes, cut into chunks

2 large fennel bulbs

6 tablespoons garlic-flavored olive oil

½–⅔ cup milk or light cream

Champ

This traditional Irish dish of potatoes and green onions or scallions is enriched with a wickedly indulgent amount of butter—for complete indulgence, replace 4 tablespoons of the milk with crème fraîche or buttermilk. Serve the champ as an accompaniment to beef or lamb stew for a warming and hearty winter meal.

SERVES FOUR

2¼ pounds potatoes, cut into chunks

1¼ cups milk

1 bunch of scallions, thinly sliced, plus extra to garnish

½ cup slightly salted butter

1 Boil the potatoes in lightly salted water for about 20–25 minutes, or until they are tender. Drain and mash the potatoes with a fork until smooth.

2 Place the milk, scallions, and half the butter in a small pan and set over low heat until just simmering. Cook for 2–3 minutes, until the butter has melted and the scallions have softened.

3 Beat the milk mixture into the mashed potato, using a wooden spoon, until the mixture is light and fluffy. Reheat gently, adding seasoning to taste.

4 Turn the potato into a warmed serving dish and make a well in the center with a spoon. Place the remaining butter in the well and let it melt. Serve immediately, sprinkled with extra scallions.

EXTRAS *To make colcannon, another Irish specialty, follow the main recipe, using half the amount of butter. Cook about 1¼ pounds finely shredded green cabbage or kale in a little water until just tender, drain thoroughly, and then beat into the creamed potato. This is delicious served with sausages and broiled ham or bacon. The colcannon may also be fried in butter and then browned under the broiler.*

Salads

WHETHER SERVED AS A MAIN COURSE OR AN
ACCOMPANIMENT, SALADS ARE ALWAYS A REFRESHING
AND WELCOME CHANGE. THE MOST SUCCESSFUL ARE
COMPOSED OF ONLY A FEW INGREDIENTS – COOKED OR
RAW – WHOSE COLORS, TEXTURES AND FLAVORS
COMPLEMENT AND BALANCE PERFECTLY.

Sour Cucumber with Fresh Dill

This is half pickle, half salad, and totally delicious served with pumpernickel or other coarse, dark, full-flavored bread, as a light meal or an appetizer. Choose smooth-skinned, small cucumbers for this recipe as larger ones tend to be less tender, with tough skins and bitter indigestible seeds. If you can only buy a large cucumber, peel it before slicing.

SERVES FOUR

1 In a large mixing bowl, combine the thinly sliced cucumbers and the thinly sliced onion. Season the vegetables with salt and toss together until they are thoroughly combined. Leave the mixture to stand in a cool place for 5–10 minutes.

2 Add the apple vinegar, 2–3 tablespoons water, and the chopped fresh dill to the cucumber and onion mixture. Toss all the ingredients together until thoroughly combined, then chill in the refrigerator for a few hours, or until ready to serve.

2 small cucumbers, thinly sliced

3 onions, thinly sliced

5–6 tablespoons apple vinegar

2–3 tablespoons chopped fresh dill

EXTRAS *For a sweet and sour mixture, add 3 tablespoons superfine sugar with the apple vinegar in step 2.*

Beet with Fresh Mint

This simple and decorative beet salad can be served as part of a selection of salads, as an appetizer, or as an accompaniment to broiled or roasted pork or lamb. Balsamic vinegar is a rich, dark vinegar with a mellow, deep flavor. It can be used to dress a variety of salad ingredients and is particularly good drizzled over a tomato and basil salad.

SERVES FOUR

1 Slice the beet or cut into even-size dice with a sharp knife. Put the beet in a bowl. Add the balsamic vinegar, olive oil, and a pinch of salt and toss together to combine.

2 Add half the thinly shredded fresh mint to the salad and toss lightly until thoroughly combined. Place the salad in the refrigerator and chill for about 1 hour. Serve garnished with the remaining thinly shredded mint leaves.

4–6 cooked beet

1–2 tablespoons balsamic vinegar

2 tablespoons olive oil

1 bunch of fresh mint, leaves stripped and thinly shredded

EXTRAS

To make Tunisian beet, add a little harissa to taste and substitute finely chopped fresh cilantro for the shredded fresh mint.

Globe Artichokes with Green Beans and Garlic Dressing

Piquant garlic dressing or creamy aioli go perfectly with these lightly-cooked vegetables. Serve lemon wedges with the artichokes so that their juice may be squeezed over to taste. The vegetables can also be garnished with finely shredded lemon rind. Artichokes should feel heavy for their size—make sure that the inner leaves are wrapped tightly round the choke and the heart inside.

SERVES FOUR TO SIX

8 ounces green beans

**3 small
globe artichokes**

**1 tablespoon lemon-
flavored olive oil**

**1 cup garlic dressing
or aioli**

1 Cook the beans in boiling water for 1–2 minutes, until slightly softened. Drain well.

2 Trim the artichoke stalks close to the base. Cook them in a large pan of salted water for about 30 minutes, or until you can easily pull away a leaf from the base. Drain well.

3 Using a sharp knife, halve them lengthwise and ease out their chokes using a teaspoon.

4 Arrange the artichokes and beans on serving plates and drizzle with the oil. Season with coarse salt and a little pepper. Spoon the garlic dressing or aioli into the hearts and serve warm.

5 To eat the artichokes, pull the leaves from the base one at a time and use to scoop a little of the dressing. It is only the fleshy end of each leaf that is eaten as well as the base, bottom, or "fond".

Halloumi and Grape Salad

Firm and salty halloumi cheese is a great standby ingredient for turning a simple salad into a special dish. In this recipe, it is tossed with sweet, juicy grapes, which complement its flavor and texture. Fresh young thyme leaves and dill taste especially good mixed with the salad. Serve with a crusty walnut or sun-dried tomato bread for a light lunch.

SERVES FOUR

1 Toss together the salad greens and fresh herb sprigs and the green and black grapes, then transfer to a large serving plate.

2 Thinly slice the halloumi cheese. Heat a large nonstick skillet. Add the sliced halloumi cheese and cook briefly until it just starts to turn golden brown on the underside. Turn the cheese with a metal spatula and cook the other side until it is golden brown.

3 Arrange the fried cheese over the salad on the plate. Pour over the oil and lemon juice or vinegar dressing and serve immediately while the cheese is still hot.

5 ounces mixed salad greens and tender fresh herb sprigs

6 ounces mixed seedless green and black grapes

9 ounces halloumi cheese

5 tablespoons oil and lemon juice or vinegar dressing

Watermelon and Feta Salad

The combination of sweet watermelon with salty feta cheese is inspired by Turkish tradition. The salad may be served plain and light, on a leafy base, or with a herbed vinaigrette dressing drizzled over. It is perfect served as an appetizer. Feta cheese is salty because it is preserved in brine—but the salt is not supposed to overpower the taste of the cheese.

SERVES FOUR

4 slices watermelon, chilled

4½ ounces feta cheese, preferably sheep's milk feta, cut into bitesize pieces

handful of mixed seeds, such as lightly toasted pumpkin seeds and sunflower seeds

10–15 black olives

1 Cut the rind off the watermelon and remove as many seeds as possible. Cut the flesh into triangular-shaped chunks.

2 Mix the watermelon, feta cheese, mixed seeds, and black olives. Cover and chill the salad for 30 minutes before serving.

COOK'S TIP *The best choice of olives for this recipe are plump black Mediterranean ones, such as kalamata, other shiny, brined varieties, or dry-cured black olives.*

Tomato, Bean, and Fried Basil Salad

Steeping basil in hot oil brings out its wonderful, aromatic flavor, which works so well in almost any tomato dish. Various canned beans can be used instead of mixed beans in this simple dish, as they all taste good and make a wholesome salad to serve as an accompaniment or a satisfying snack with some warm, grainy bread.

SERVES FOUR

1 Reserve a third of the basil leaves for garnish, then tear the remainder into pieces. Pour the olive oil into a small pan. Add the torn basil and heat gently for 1 minute, until the basil sizzles and begins to color.

2 Place the halved cherry tomatoes and beans in a bowl. Pour in the basil oil and add a little salt and plenty of freshly ground black pepper. Toss the ingredients together gently, cover, and marinate at room temperature for at least 30 minutes. Serve the salad sprinkled with the remaining basil leaves.

½ cup fresh basil leaves

5 tablespoons extra virgin olive oil

11 ounces cherry tomatoes, halved

14-ounce can mixed beans, drained and rinsed

Moroccan Date, Orange, and Carrot Salad

Take exotic fresh dates and marry them with everyday ingredients, such as carrots and oranges, to make this deliciously different salad. The salad looks really pretty arranged on a base of sweet Bibb lettuce leaves. This fruity salad is excellent served with charbroiled lamb steaks, or with skewered lamb.

SERVES FOUR

3 carrots

3 oranges

4 ounces fresh dates, pitted and cut lengthwise into eighths

¼ cup toasted whole almonds, chopped

1 Grate the carrots and place in a mound in a serving dish, or on four individual plates.

2 Peel and segment two of the oranges and arrange the orange segments around the carrot. Season with salt and freshly ground black pepper. Pile the dates on top, then sprinkle with the chopped, toasted almonds.

3 Squeeze the juice from the remaining orange and sprinkle it over the salad. Chill in the refrigerator for an hour before serving.

Pink Grapefruit and Avocado Salad

Smooth, creamy avocado and zesty citrus fruit are perfect partners in an attractive, refreshing salad. Pink grapefruit are tangy but not too sharp, or try large oranges for a sweeter flavor. Avocados turn brown quickly when exposed to the air: the acidic grapefruit juice will prevent this from occurring, so combine the ingredients as soon as the avocados have been sliced.

SERVES FOUR

1 Slice the top and bottom off one grapefruit, then cut off all the peel and pith from around the side. Working over a small bowl to catch the juices, cut out the segments from between the membranes and place them in a separate bowl. Squeeze any juices remaining in the membranes into the bowl, then discard them. Repeat with the remaining grapefruit.

2 Halve, pit, and peel the avocados. Slice the flesh and add it to the prepared grapefruit segments. Whisk a little salt and then the chili oil into the grapefruit juice.

3 Pile the arugula leaves onto four serving plates and top with the grapefruit segments and avocado. Pour over the dressing and serve. Alternatively, toss the arugula with the grapefruit, avocado, and dressing, then divide the salad among plates or bowls.

2 pink grapefruit

2 ripe avocados

2 tablespoons chili oil

3½ ounces arugula

Turnip Salad in Sour Cream

Usually served cooked, raw young tender turnips which are sliced or grated in this recipe have a tangy, slightly peppery flavor. Serve this unusual salad as an accompaniment for broiled poultry or meat. It is also delicious as a light appetizer served with warmed flat breads, such as pita or nan. Garnish the salad with fresh flat leaf parsley and paprika, if you like.

SERVES FOUR

1 Thinly slice or coarsely grate the turnips. Alternatively, thinly slice half the turnips and grate the remaining half. Put in a bowl.

2 Add the onion and vinegar and season to taste with salt and plenty of freshly ground black pepper. Toss together, then stir in the sour cream. Chill well before serving.

VARIATIONS
Large white radishes can be used instead of turnips and crème fraîche can be substituted for the sour cream. The salad is good with a selection of salads and cold dishes for a light lunch or long and leisurely supper.

2–4 young, tender turnips, peeled

¼–½ onion, finely chopped

2–3 drops white wine vinegar, or to taste

4–6 tablespoons sour cream

Moroccan Carrot Salad

In this intriguing salad from North Africa, the carrots are lightly cooked before being tossed in a cumin and cilantro vinaigrette. Cumin is widely used in Indian and Mexican cooking, as well as North African cuisines. It has a strong and spicy aroma and a warm pungent flavor that goes particularly well with root vegetables. This salad is a perfect accompaniment for both everyday or special meals.

SERVES FOUR TO SIX

3–4 carrots, thinly sliced

¼ teaspoon ground cumin, or to taste

4 tablespoons garlic-flavored oil and vinegar dressing

2 tablespoons chopped fresh cilantro leaves or a mixture of cilantro and parsley

1 Cook the thinly sliced carrots by either steaming or boiling in lightly salted water until they are just tender but not soft. Drain the carrots, leave for a few minutes to dry and cool, then put into a mixing bowl.

2 Add the cumin, garlic dressing, and herbs. Season to taste and chill well before serving. Check the seasoning just before serving and add more ground cumin, salt, or black pepper, if required.

Warm Chorizo and Spinach Salad

Spanish chorizo sausage contributes an intense spiciness to any ingredient with which it is cooked. In this hearty warm salad, spinach has sufficient flavor to compete with the chorizo. Watercress or arugula could be used instead of the spinach, if you prefer. For an added dimension use a flavored olive oil—rosemary, garlic, or chili oil would work perfectly. Serve the salad with warm crusty bread to soak up all the delicious cooking juices.

SERVES FOUR

1 Discard any tough stalks from the spinach. Pour the oil into a large skillet and add the sausage. Cook gently for 3 minutes, until the sausage slices start to shrivel slightly and color.

2 Add the spinach leaves and remove the skillet from the heat. Toss the spinach in the warm oil until it just starts to wilt. Add the sherry vinegar and a little seasoning. Toss the ingredients briefly, then serve immediately, while still warm.

8 ounces baby spinach leaves

6 tablespoons extra virgin olive oil

5 ounces chorizo sausage, very thinly sliced

2 tablespoons sherry vinegar

Potato and Olive Salad

This delicious salad is simple and zesty—the perfect choice for lunch, as an accompaniment, or as an appetizer. Similar in appearance to flat leaf parsley, fresh cilantro has a distinctive pungent, almost spicy flavor. It is widely used in India, the Middle and Far East, and in eastern Mediterranean countries. This potato salad is particularly good served as part of a brunch.

SERVES FOUR

8 large new potatoes

3–4 tablespoons garlic-flavored oil and vinegar dressing

4–6 tablespoons chopped fresh herbs, such as cilantro and chives

10–15 dry-fleshed black Mediterranean olives

1 Cut the new potatoes into chunks. Put them in a pan, pour in water to cover, and add a pinch of salt. Bring to a boil, then reduce the heat, and cook gently for about 10 minutes, or until the potatoes are just tender. Drain well and leave in a colander to dry thoroughly and cool slightly.

2 When they are cool enough to handle, chop the potatoes and put them in a serving bowl.

3 Drizzle the garlic dressing over the potatoes. Toss well and sprinkle with the chopped fresh cilantro and chives, and black olives. Chill in the refrigerator for at least 1 hour before serving.

EXTRAS *Add a pinch of ground cumin or a sprinkling of roasted whole cumin seeds to spice up the salad.*

Asparagus, Bacon, and Leaf Salad

This excellent salad turns a plain roast chicken or simple broiled fish into an interesting meal, especially when served with buttered new potatoes. It also makes an appetizing first course or light lunch. A wide range of different salad greens are readily available—frisée has feathery, curly, slightly bitter-tasting leaves and is a member of the same family as Belgian endive and radicchio. Frisée leaves range in color from yellow-white to yellow-green.

SERVES FOUR

1 Trim off any tough stalk ends from the asparagus and cut the spears into three, setting the tender tips aside. Heat a ½-inch depth of water in a skillet until simmering. Reserve the asparagus tips and cook the remainder of the spears in the water for about 3 minutes, until almost tender. Add the tips and cook for 1 minute more. Drain and refresh under cold, running water.

2 Dry-fry the bacon until golden and crisp and then set it aside to cool slightly. Use kitchen scissors to snip it into bitesize pieces. Place the frisée or mixed salad greens in a bowl and add the bacon.

3 Add the asparagus and a little black pepper to the salad. Pour the dressing over and toss the salad lightly, then serve before the leaves begin to wilt.

1¼ pounds medium asparagus spears

4½ ounces thin-cut smoked lean bacon

9 ounces frisée lettuce leaves or mixed salad greens

scant ½ cup French dressing

Anchovy and Roasted Bell Pepper Salad

Sweet bell peppers, salty anchovies, and plenty of garlic make an intensely flavored salad that is delicious with meat, poultry, or cheese. It also makes a tasty snack with olive bread. If you find that canned anchovies are too salty for your liking, you can reduce their saltiness by soaking them in milk for 20 minutes. Drain off the oil first and after soaking, drain and rinse them in cold water.

SERVES FOUR

**2 red, 2 orange and
2 yellow bell peppers,
halved and seeded**

**2-ounce can anchovies
in olive oil**

2 garlic cloves

**3 tablespoons
balsamic vinegar**

1 Preheat the oven to 400°F. Place the bell peppers, cut side down, in a roasting pan. Roast for 30-40 minutes, until the skins are charred. Transfer the bell peppers to a bowl, cover with plastic wrap, and leave for 15 minutes.

2 Peel the bell peppers, then cut them into chunky strips. Drain the anchovies, reserving the oil, and halve the fillets lengthwise.

3 Slice the garlic as thinly as possible and place it in a large bowl. Stir in the reserved oil, vinegar, and a little pepper. Add the bell peppers and anchovies and use a spoon and fork to fold the ingredients together. Cover and chill until ready to serve.

Ice Creams and Frozen Desserts

ICE CREAMS AND ICED DESSERTS CAN MAKE A PERFECT,
REFRESHING END TO A MEAL. HOME-MADE ICES, WHETHER
A LIGHTLY PERFUMED SORBET, A CREAMY KULFI OR A RICH
AND CREAMY ICE CREAM GÂTEAU, ARE SURPRISINGLY
EASY TO MAKE AND A WONDERFUL TREAT TO SERVE
TO GUESTS AND FAMILY ALIKE.

Lemon Sherbet

This is probably the most classic sherbet of all. Refreshingly tangy and yet deliciously smooth, it quite literally melts in the mouth. Try to buy unwaxed lemons for recipes where the lemon rind is used. The wax coating can adversely affect the flavor of the rind.

SERVES SIX

1 cup superfine sugar, plus extra for coating rind to decorate

4 lemons, well scrubbed

1 egg white

1 Put the sugar in a pan and pour in 1¼ cups water. Bring to a boil, stirring occasionally until the sugar has just dissolved.

2 Using a swivel vegetable peeler, pare the rind thinly from two of the lemons so that it falls straight into the pan.

3 Simmer for 2 minutes, without stirring, then take the pan off the heat. Let cool, then chill.

4 Squeeze the juice from all the lemons and add it to the syrup. Strain the syrup into a shallow freezerproof container, reserving the rind. Freeze the mixture for 4 hours, until it is mushy.

5 Process the sherbet in a food processor until it is smooth. Lightly whisk the egg white with a fork until it is just frothy. Replace the sherbet in the container, beat in the egg white, and return the mixture to the freezer for 4 hours, or until it is firm.

6 Cut the reserved lemon rind into fine shreds and cook them in boiling water for 5 minutes, or until tender. Drain, then place on a plate, and sprinkle generously with superfine sugar. Scoop the sherbet into bowls or glasses and decorate with the sugared lemon rind.

Strawberry and Lavender Sherbet

A hint of lavender transforms a familiar strawberry sherbet into a perfumed dinner-party dessert. When buying strawberries, look for plump, shiny fruit without any signs of straining or leakage at the base of the container—this suggests that the fruit at the bottom has been squashed. To hull strawberries, prize out the leafy top with a sharp knife or a specially designed strawberry huller.

SERVES SIX

1 Place the sugar in a pan and pour in 1¼ cups water. Bring to a boil, stirring until the sugar has dissolved.

2 Take the pan off the heat, add the lavender flowers, and set aside to steep for 1 hour. If time permits, chill the syrup in the refrigerator before using.

3 Process the strawberries in a food processor or in batches in a blender, then press the purée through a large strainer into a bowl.

4 Pour the purée into a freezerproof container, strain in the syrup, and freeze for 4 hours, or until mushy. Transfer to a food processor and process until smooth. Whisk the egg white until frothy, and stir into the sherbet. Spoon the sherbet back into the container and freeze until firm.

5 Serve in scoops, piled into tall glasses, and decorate with sprigs of lavender flowers.

¾ cup superfine sugar

6 fresh lavender flowers, plus extra to decorate

5 cups strawberries, hulled

1 egg white

COOK'S TIP
The size of the lavender flowers can vary; if they are very small, you may need to use eight. To double check, taste a little of the cooled lavender syrup. If you think the flavor is too mild, add two or three more flowers, reheat, and cool again before using.

Black Currant Sherbet

Wonderfully sharp and bursting with flavor, black currants make a really fabulous sherbet. Black currants are more acidic than white or red currants and are very rarely eaten raw. Taste the mixture after adding the syrup, and if you find it a little too sharp, add a little more sugar before freezing.

5 cups black currants, trimmed, plus extra to decorate

¼ cup superfine sugar

1 egg white

SERVES SIX

1 Put the black currants in a pan and add ⅔ cup water. Cover the pan and simmer for 5 minutes, or until the fruit is soft. Cool, then process to a purée in a food processor or blender.

2 Set a large strainer over a bowl, pour the purée into the strainer, then press it through the mesh with the back of a spoon to form a smooth liquid.

3 Pour scant 1 cup water into a clean pan. Add the sugar and bring to a boil, stirring until the sugar has dissolved. Pour the syrup into a bowl. Cool, then chill.

4 Mix the black currant purée and sugar syrup together. Spoon into a freezerproof container and freeze until mushy. Lightly whisk the egg white until just frothy. Process the sherbet in a food processor until smooth, then return it to the container, and stir in the egg white. Freeze for 4 hours, or until firm.

5 Transfer the sherbet to the refrigerator about 15 minutes before serving. Serve in scoops, decorated with the black currant sprigs.

Damson Water Ice

Perfectly ripe damsons are sharp and full of flavor—if you can't find damsons, use another deep-red variety of plum or extra-juicy Victoria plums. To add an extra, nutty flavor to this mouthwatering ice, serve sprinkled with finely chopped toasted almonds.

SERVES SIX

1¼ pounds ripe damsons, washed

¾ cup superfine sugar

1 Put the damsons into a pan and add ⅔ cup water. Cover and simmer gently for 10 minutes, or until the damsons are tender.

2 Pour 1¼ cups water into a second pan. Add the sugar and bring to a boil, stirring until the sugar has dissolved. Pour the syrup into a bowl, let cool, then chill.

3 Break up the cooked damsons in the pan with a wooden spoon and scoop out any free pits. Pour the fruit and juices into a large strainer set over a bowl. Press the fruit through the strainer and discard the skins and any remaining pits from the strainer.

4 Pour the damson purée into a shallow plastic container. Stir in the syrup and freeze for 6 hours, beating once or twice to break up the ice crystals.

5 Spoon into tall serving glasses or dishes and serve the water ice with wafers.

VARIATION

Apricot water ice can be made in exactly the same way. Flavor the water ice with a little lemon or orange rind or add a broken cinnamon stick to the pan when poaching the fruit. Serve garnished with sprigs of mint or nasturtium flowers.

Peach and Cardamom Yogurt Ice

Make the most of spices that are familiar in savory cooking by discovering their potential for sweet dishes. Cardamom, often used in Indian cookery, has a warm pungent aroma and a subtle lemon flavor. Although it is made with yogurt rather than cream, this ice cream has a luxurious velvety texture and it is a healthy choice, too.

SERVES FOUR

8 cardamom pods

6 peaches, total weight about 1¼ pounds, halved and pitted

6 tablespoons superfine sugar

scant 1 cup plain yogurt

1 Put the cardamom pods on a board and crush them with the base of a ramekin, or place in a mortar and crush with a pestle.

2 Chop the peaches coarsely and put them in a pan. Add the crushed cardamom pods, with their black seeds, the sugar, and 2 tablespoons water. Cover and simmer for 10 minutes, or until the fruit is tender. Let cool.

3 Process the peach mixture in a food processor or blender until smooth, then press through a strainer placed over a bowl.

4 Mix the yogurt into the strained purée and pour into a freezerproof container. Freeze for 5–6 hours, until firm, beating once or twice with a fork, electric whisk, or in a processor to break up the ice crystals.

5 Scoop the ice cream onto a large platter and serve.

Blackberry Ice Cream

There could scarcely be fewer ingredients in this delicious, vibrant ice cream, which is simple to make and ideal as a prepare-ahead dessert. Serve the ice cream with cookies, such as shortbread or almond cookies, to provide a delicious contrast in taste and texture.

SERVES FOUR TO SIX

5 cups blackberries, hulled, plus extra to decorate

6 tablespoons superfine sugar

1¼ cups whipping cream

crisp dessert cookies, to serve

COOK'S TIP

Frozen blackberries can be used instead of fresh. You will need to increase the cooking time to 10 minutes and stir occasionally.

1 Put the blackberries into a pan, add 2 tablespoons water and the sugar. Cover and simmer for 5 minutes, until just soft.

2 Tip the fruit into a strainer placed over a bowl and press it through the mesh, using a wooden spoon. Let cool, then chill.

3 Whip the cream until it is just thick but still soft enough to fall from a spoon, then mix it with the chilled fruit purée. Pour the mixture into a freezerproof container and freeze for 2 hours, or until it is part frozen.

4 Mash the mixture with a fork or process it in a food processor to break up the ice crystals. Return it to the freezer for 4 hours more, mashing or processing the mixture again after 2 hours.

5 Scoop the ice cream into dishes and decorate with extra blackberries. Serve with crisp dessert cookies.

Kulfi

This favorite Indian ice cream is traditionally made by carefully boiling milk until it has reduced to about one-third of its original quantity. Although you can save time by using condensed milk, nothing beats the luscious result achieved by using the authentic method. When they are available, rose petals are a stylish decoration in addition to the pistachios.

6¼ cups whole milk

3 cardamom pods

2 tablespoons
superfine sugar

½ cup pistachio nuts, skinned

SERVES FOUR

1 Pour the milk into a large, heavy pan. Bring to a boil, reduce the heat, and simmer gently for 1 hour, stirring occasionally.

2 Put the cardamom pods in a mortar and crush them with a pestle. Add the pods and the seeds to the milk and continue to simmer, stirring frequently, for 1–1½ hours, or until the milk has reduced to about 2 cups. Strain the milk into a pitcher, stir in the sugar, and let cool.

3 Grind half the pistachios in a blender or nut grinder. Cut the remaining pistachios into thin slivers and set them aside for decoration. Stir the ground nuts into the milk mixture.

4 Pour the milk and pistachio mixture into four kulfi or popsicle molds. Freeze the mixture overnight, or until firm.

5 To unmold the kulfi, half fill a plastic container or bowl with very hot water, stand the molds in the water, and count to ten. Immediately lift out the molds and invert them onto a cookie sheet. Transfer the ice creams to individual plates and sprinkle sliced pistachios over the top.

Coconut Ice

The creamy taste and texture of this ice cream comes from the natural fat content of coconut as the mixture contains neither cream nor egg and is very refreshing. The lime adds a delicious tangy flavor as well as pretty green specks to the finished ice. Decorate with toasted coconut shavings or toasted dry unsweetened shredded coconut (this browns very quickly, so watch it constantly).

SERVES FOUR TO SIX

generous ½ cup superfine sugar

2 limes

1¾ cups canned coconut milk

toasted coconut shavings, to decorate (optional)

1 Pour ⅔ cup water into a small pan. Tip in the superfine sugar and bring to a boil, stirring constantly until the sugar has completely dissolved. Remove the pan from the heat and let the syrup cool, then chill well.

2 Grate the rind from the limes finely, taking care to avoid the bitter pith. Squeeze out their juice and add to the pan of syrup with the rind. Add the coconut milk.

3 Pour the mixture into a freezerproof container and freeze for 5–6 hours, or until firm. Beat twice with a fork or electric whisk, or process in a food processor to break up the crystals. Scoop into dishes and decorate with toasted coconut shavings, if you like.

COOK'S TIP *To make toasted coconut shavings, rinse the flesh from a coconut under cold water. Shave thin slices using a vegetable peeler, then toast under a moderate broiler until they are curled and the edges have turned golden.*

Gingered Semi-freddo

This Italian ice cream is rather like the original soft scoop ice cream. Made with a boiled sugar syrup rather than a traditional egg custard, and generously speckled with chopped preserved ginger, this delicious ice cream will stay soft when frozen. For a really impressive dinner party dessert, serve the semi-freddo in semisweet chocolate cases.

SERVES SIX

1 Mix the sugar and ½ cup cold water in a pan and heat gently, stirring occasionally, until the sugar has dissolved.

2 Increase the heat and boil for 4–5 minutes, without stirring, until the syrup registers 238°F on a sugar thermometer. Alternatively, test by dropping a little of the syrup into a cup of cold water. Pour the water away and you should be able to mold the syrup into a small ball.

3 Put the egg yolks in a large heatproof bowl and whisk until frothy. Place the bowl over a pan of simmering water and whisk in the sugar syrup. Continue whisking until the mixture is very thick. Remove from the heat and whisk until cool.

4 Whip the cream and lightly fold it into the egg yolk mixture with the chopped preserved ginger. Pour into a freezerproof container and freeze for 1 hour.

5 Stir the semi-freddo to bring any ginger that has sunk to the base of the container to the top, then return it to the freezer for 5–6 hours, until firm. Scoop into dishes or chocolate cases (*see* Cook's Tip). Decorate with slices of ginger and serve.

generous ½ cup superfine sugar

4 egg yolks

1¼ cups heavy cream

⅔ cup drained preserved ginger, finely chopped, plus extra slices, to decorate

COOK'S TIP *To make the cases, pour melted chocolate over squares of baking parchment and drape them over upturned glasses. Peel off the baking parchment when set.*

Miniature Choc-ices

These little chocolate-coated ice creams make a fun alternative to the more familiar after-dinner chocolates, especially on hot summer evenings—although they need to be eaten quickly. Serve the choc-ices in fluted paper candy cases. If you can, buy gold cases as they will contrast very prettily with the dark chocolate coating.

MAKES ABOUT TWENTY-FIVE

3 cups vanilla, chocolate, or coffee ice cream

7 ounces semisweet chocolate, broken into pieces

1 ounce milk chocolate, broken into pieces

¼ cup finely chopped hazelnuts, lightly toasted

1 Put a large cookie sheet in the freezer for 10 minutes. Using a melon baller, scoop balls of ice cream and place these on the cookie sheet. Freeze for at least 1 hour, or until firm.

2 Line a second cookie sheet with baking parchment and place in the freezer for 15 minutes. Melt the semisweet chocolate in a heatproof bowl set over a pan of gently simmering water. Melt the milk chocolate in a separate bowl.

3 Using a metal spatula, transfer the ice cream scoops to the parchment-lined sheet. Spoon a little semisweet chocolate over one scoop so that most of it is coated.

4 Sprinkle immediately with chopped nuts, before the chocolate sets. Coat half the remaining scoops in the same way, sprinkling each one with nuts before the chocolate sets. Spoon the remaining semisweet chocolate over all the remaining scoops.

5 Using a teaspoon, drizzle the milk chocolate over the choc-ices that are not topped with nuts. Freeze again until ready to serve.

White Chocolate Castles

With a little ingenuity, good-quality bought ice cream can masquerade as a culinary masterpiece—it's down to perfect presentation. For a professional finish, dust the castles and plates with a hint of unsweetened cocoa powder or confectioners' sugar.

8 ounces white chocolate, broken into pieces

1 cup white chocolate ice cream

1 cup dark chocolate ice cream

1 cup berries

SERVES SIX

1 Put the white chocolate in a heatproof bowl, set it over a pan of gently simmering water, and leave until melted. Line a cookie sheet with waxed paper. Cut out six 12 x 5 inch strips of waxed paper, then fold each in half lengthwise.

2 Stand a 3-inch cookie cutter on the cookie sheet. Roll one strip of paper into a circle and fit it inside the cutter with the folded edge on the base paper. Stick the edges together with tape.

3 Remove the cutter and shape more paper collars in the same way, leaving the cookie cutter in place around the final collar.

4 Spoon a little of the melted chocolate into the base of the collar supported by the cutter. Using a teaspoon, spread the chocolate over the base and up the sides of the collar, making the top edge uneven. Carefully lift away the cutter.

5 Make five more chocolate cases in the same way, using the cutter for extra support each time. Leave the cases in a cool place or in the refrigerator to set.

6 Carefully peel away the paper from the sides of the chocolate cases, then lift the cases off the base. Transfer to serving plates.

7 Using a large melon baller or teaspoon, scoop the white and dark chocolate ice creams into the cases and decorate with berries. Serve immediately.

Caramel and Pecan Terrine

Frozen or long-life cream is a useful ingredient for making impressive desserts without having a mega shopping trip. Caramel and nuts transform cream to parfait in this recipe. Take care that the syrup does not become too dark, or the ice cream will taste bitter.

SERVES SIX

generous ½ cup sugar

scant 2 cups heavy cream

2 tablespoons confectioners' sugar

¾ cup pecan nuts, toasted

COOK'S TIP *Watch the caramel syrup closely after removing it from the heat. If it starts to turn too dark, dip the base of the pan in cold water. If the syrup remains very pale, return the pan to the heat and cook it for a little longer.*

1 Heat the sugar and 5 tablespoons water in a small, heavy pan until the sugar dissolves. Boil rapidly until the sugar has turned pale golden. Remove the pan from the heat and let stand until the syrup turns a rich brown color.

2 Pour 6 tablespoons of the cream over the caramel. Heat to make a smooth sauce. Let cool.

3 Rinse a 1-pound loaf pan, then line the base and sides with plastic wrap. Whip a further ⅔ cup of the cream with the confectioners' sugar until it forms soft peaks. Whip the remaining cream separately and stir in the caramel sauce and the toasted pecan nuts.

4 Spoon one-third of the caramel cream into the prepared pan and spread with half the plain whipped cream. Spread half of the remaining caramel cream over the top, then top with the remaining plain cream. Finally, add the remaining caramel cream and level the surface. Freeze for 6 hours.

5 To serve, dip the pan in very hot water for 2 seconds, invert it onto a serving plate, and peel away the lining. Serve sliced.

White Chocolate and Brownie Torte

This delicious dessert is easy to make and guaranteed to appeal to just about everyone. If you can't buy good quality brownies, use a moist chocolate sponge cake or make your own. For extra decoration, put a few fresh summer berries around the edge or on the center of the torte.

SERVES TEN

11 ounces white chocolate, broken into pieces

2½ cups heavy cream

9 ounces rich chocolate brownies

unsweetened cocoa powder, for dusting

1 Dampen the sides of an 8-inch springform pan and line with a strip of waxed paper. Put the chocolate in a small pan. Add ⅔ cup of the cream and heat very gently until the chocolate has melted. Stir until smooth, then pour into a bowl, and let cool.

2 Break the chocolate brownies into chunky pieces and sprinkle these over the base of the pan. Pack them down lightly to make a fairly dense base.

3 Whip the remaining cream until it forms peaks, then fold in the white chocolate mixture. Spoon into the pan to cover the layer of brownies, then tap the pan gently on the counter to level the chocolate mixture. Cover and freeze overnight.

4 Transfer the torte to the refrigerator about 45 minutes before serving to soften slightly. Decorate with a light dusting of unsweetened cocoa powder just before serving.

Soft Fruit and Meringue Cake

This recipe takes only five minutes to prepare but looks and tastes as though a lot of preparation went into it. The trick is to use really good vanilla ice cream. For a dinner party, slice the cake and place on individual plates, spoon ready-made strawberry or raspberry coulis around each slice, and garnish with whole strawberries or raspberries.

SERVES SIX

1 Dampen a 2-pound loaf pan and line it with plastic wrap. If using strawberries, chop them into small pieces. Put them in a bowl and add the raspberries or red currants and confectioners' sugar. Toss gently until the fruit is beginning to break up, but do not let it become mushy.

2 Put the ice cream in a bowl and break it up with a fork. Crumble the meringues into the bowl and add the soft fruit mixture.

3 Fold all the ingredients together until evenly combined and lightly marbled. Pack into the prepared pan and press down gently to level. Cover and freeze overnight. To serve, invert onto a plate and peel away the plastic wrap. Serve in slices.

3½ cups mixed small strawberries, raspberries, and/ or red currants

2 tablespoons confectioners' sugar

3 cups vanilla ice cream

6 meringue nests or 4 ounces meringue

Cold Desserts

BECAUSE THEY CAN BE MADE IN ADVANCE, COLD DESSERTS

ARE THE PERFECT CHOICE FOR ENTERTAINING. ALL THE

RECIPES IN THIS CHAPTER HAVE AN ELEGANT SIMPLICITY

THAT GUARANTEES SUCCESS WITH EVEN THE MOST

SOPHISTICATED DINNER GUESTS. HOWEVER, THESE

DESSERTS ARE SO EASY TO PREPARE THAT YOU WILL WANT

TO SERVE THEM FOR EVERYDAY MEALS TOO.

Tropical-scented Fruit Salad

With its special color and exotic flavor, this fresh fruit salad is perfect after a rich, heavy meal. For fabulous flavor and color, try using three small blood oranges and three ordinary oranges. Other fruit that can be added include pears, kiwi fruit, and bananas. Serve the fruit salad with whipping cream flavored with ½ ounce finely chopped drained preserved stem ginger.

SERVES FOUR TO SIX

1 Put the hulled and halved strawberries and peeled and segmented oranges into a serving bowl. Halve the passion fruit and, using a teaspoon, scoop the flesh into the bowl.

2 Pour the wine over the fruit and toss gently. Cover and chill in the refrigerator until ready to serve.

3–3½ cups strawberries, hulled and halved

6 oranges, peeled and segmented

1–2 passion fruit

½ cup medium dry or sweet white wine

Juniper-scented Pears in Red Wine

More often used in savory dishes than sweet, juniper berries have a dark blue, almost black color with a distinct gin-like flavor. In this fruity winter dessert, crushed juniper berries give the classic partnership of pears and red wine a slightly aromatic flavor. These pears are particularly good sprinkled with toasted almonds and whipped cream.

SERVES FOUR

1 Lightly crush the juniper berries using a pestle and mortar or with the end of a rolling pin. Put the berries in a pan with the sugar and wine and heat gently until the sugar dissolves.

2 Meanwhile, peel the pears, leaving them whole. Add them to the wine and heat until just simmering. Cover the pan and cook gently for about 25 minutes, until the pears are tender. Turn the pears once or twice to make sure they cook evenly.

3 Use a slotted spoon to remove the pears. Boil the syrup hard for a few minutes, until it is slightly reduced and thickened. If serving the pears hot, reheat them gently in the syrup, otherwise arrange them in a serving dish and spoon the syrup over.

2 tablespoons juniper berries

¼ cup superfine sugar

2½ cups red wine

4 large or 8 small firm pears, stalks intact

Oranges in Syrup

This recipe works well with most citrus fruits—for example, try pink grapefruit or sweet, perfumed clementines, which have been peeled but left whole. Serve the oranges with 1¼ cups whipped cream flavored with 1 teaspoon ground cinnamon or with 1 teaspoon ground nutmeg or with strained plain yogurt.

SERVES SIX

6 medium oranges

1 cup sugar

scant ½ cup fresh strong brewed coffee

½ cup pistachio nuts, chopped (optional)

1 Finely pare, shred, and reserve the rind from one orange. Peel the remaining oranges. Cut each one crosswise into slices, then re-form them, with a toothpick through the center.

2 Put the sugar in a heavy pan and add ¼ cup water. Heat gently until the sugar dissolves, then bring to a boil, and cook until the syrup turns pale gold.

3 Remove from the heat and carefully pour scant ½ cup freshly boiling water into the pan. Return to the heat until the syrup has dissolved in the water. Stir in the coffee.

4 Add the oranges and the rind to the coffee syrup. Simmer for 15–20 minutes, turning the oranges once during cooking. Leave to cool, then chill. Serve sprinkled with pistachio nuts, if using.

COOK'S TIP *Choose a pan in which the oranges will just fit in a single layer—use a deep skillet if you don't have a pan that is large enough.*

Fresh Fig Compote

A vanilla and coffee syrup brings out the wonderful flavor of figs—serve strained plain yogurt or vanilla ice cream with the poached fruit. A good selection of different honey is available—its aroma and flavor will be subtly scented by the plants surrounding the hives. Orange blossom honey works particularly well in this recipe, although any clear variety is suitable.

SERVES FOUR TO SIX

1⅔ cups fresh brewed coffee

½ cup honey

1 vanilla bean

12 slightly under-ripe fresh figs

1 Choose a skillet with a lid, large enough to hold the figs in a single layer. Pour in the coffee and add the honey.

2 Split the vanilla bean lengthwise and scrape the seeds into the pan. Add the vanilla bean then bring to a rapid boil, and cook until reduced to about ¾ cup.

3 Wash the figs and pierce the skins several times with a sharp skewer. Cut in half and add to the syrup. Reduce the heat, cover, and simmer for 5 minutes. Remove the figs from the syrup with a slotted spoon and set aside to cool.

4 Strain the syrup over the figs. Let stand at room temperature for 1 hour before serving.

COOK'S TIP *Figs come in three main varieties— red, white and black—and all three are suitable for cooking. They are sweet and succulent, and complement the stronger, more pervasive flavors of coffee and vanilla very well.*

Baked Custard with Burnt Sugar

This delicious egg custard or crème brûlée is a rich indulgent dessert that can be prepared well in advance. You can buy vanilla sugar or make your own by placing a split vanilla bean in a jar of superfine sugar—the sugar will be ready to use after a couple of days.

SERVES SIX

1 Preheat the oven to 300°F. Place six ½-cup ramekins in a roasting pan or large ovenproof dish and set aside while you prepare the vanilla custard.

2 Heat the heavy cream in a heavy pan over gentle heat until it is very hot, but not boiling.

3 In a bowl, whisk the egg yolks and vanilla sugar until well blended. Whisk in the hot cream and strain into a large pitcher. Divide the custard equally among the ramekins.

4 Pour enough boiling water into the roasting pan to come about halfway up the sides of the ramekins. Cover the pan with foil and bake for about 30 minutes, until the custards are just set. (Push the point of a knife into the centre of one; if it comes out clean, the custards are cooked.) Remove the ramekins from the pan, leave to cool, then chill.

5 Preheat the broiler. Sprinkle the brown sugar evenly over the surface of the custards and broil for 30–60 seconds, until the sugar melts and caramelizes, taking care not to let it burn. Place in the refrigerator to chill and set the crust.

4 cups heavy cream

6 egg yolks

½ cup vanilla sugar

⅓ cup soft light brown sugar

COOK'S TIP

It is best to make the custards the day before you wish to eat them and chill overnight, so that they are really cold and firm.

Passion Fruit Creams

These delicately perfumed creams are light with a fresh flavor from the passion fruit. Ripe passion fruit should look purple and wrinkled—choose fruit that are heavy for their size. When halved, the fragrant, sweet juicy flesh with small edible black seeds are revealed. These creams can be decorated with mint or geranium leaves and served with cream.

SERVES FIVE TO SIX

1 Preheat the oven to 350°F. Line the bases of six ½-cup ramekins with rounds of baking parchment and place them in a roasting pan.

2 Heat the cream to just below boiling point, then remove the pan from the heat. Sift the flesh of four passion fruits and beat together with the sugar and eggs. Whisk in the hot cream and then ladle into the ramekins.

3 Half fill the roasting pan with boiling water. Bake the creams for 25–30 minutes, or until set, then let cool before chilling.

4 Run a knife around the insides of the ramekins, then invert them onto serving plates, tapping the bases firmly. Carefully peel off the baking parchment and chill in the refrigerator until ready to serve. Spoon on a little passion fruit flesh just before serving.

2½ cups heavy cream, or a mixture of light and heavy cream

6 passion fruits

2–3 tablespoons vanilla sugar

5 eggs

Baked Caramel Custard

Many countries have their own version of this classic dessert. Known as *crème caramel* in France and *flan* in Spain, this chilled baked custard has a rich caramel flavor. By cooking the custard in a *bain marie* or, as here, in a roasting pan with water, the mixture is cooked gently and the eggs are prevented from becoming tough or curdling. It is delicious served with strawberries and thick cream.

SERVES SIX TO EIGHT

1 Put generous ¾ cup of the sugar in a small heavy pan with just enough water to moisten the sugar. Bring to a boil over high heat, swirling the pan until the sugar has dissolved completely. Boil for about 5 minutes, without stirring, until the syrup turns a dark caramel color.

2 Working quickly, pour the caramel into a 4-cup soufflé dish. Holding the dish with potholders, carefully swirl it to coat the base and sides with the hot caramel mixture. Set aside to cool.

3 Preheat the oven to 325°F. In a bowl, whisk the eggs and egg yolks with the remaining sugar for 2–3 minutes, until smooth and creamy.

4 Heat the cream in a heavy pan until hot, but not boiling. Whisk the hot cream into the egg mixture and carefully strain the mixture into the caramel-lined dish. Cover tightly with foil.

5 Place the dish in a roasting pan and pour in just enough boiling water to come halfway up the side of the dish. Bake the custard for 40–45 minutes, until just set. To test whether the custard is set, insert a knife about 2 inches from the edge; if the blade comes out clean, the custard should be ready.

6 Remove the soufflé dish from the roasting pan and let cool for at least 30 minutes, then place in the refrigerator, and chill overnight.

7 To turn out, carefully run a sharp knife around the edge of the dish to loosen the custard. Cover the dish with a serving plate and, holding them both together very tightly, invert the dish and plate, letting the custard drop down onto the plate.

8 Gently lift one edge of the dish, allowing the caramel to run down over the sides and onto the plate, then carefully lift off the dish. Serve immediately.

1¼ cups vanilla sugar

5 extra large eggs, plus 2 extra yolks

scant 2 cups heavy cream

VARIATION

For a special occasion, make individual baked custards in ramekin dishes. Coat six to eight ramekins with the caramel and divide the custard mixture among them. Bake, in a roasting pan of water, for 25–30 minutes, or until set. Thinly slice the strawberries and marinate them in a little sugar and a liqueur or dessert wine, such as Amaretto or Muscat wine.

Chilled Chocolate and Espresso Mousse

Heady, aromatic espresso coffee adds a distinctive flavor to this smooth, rich mousse. For a special occasion, serve the mousse in stylish chocolate cups decorated with sprigs of mint, with mascarpone or thick cream on the side.

SERVES FOUR

**1 pound
semisweet chocolate**

**3 tablespoons freshly
brewed espresso**

**2 tablespoons
sweet butter**

4 eggs, separated

1 For each chocolate cup, cut a double thickness 6-inch square of foil. Mold it around a small orange, leaving the edges and corners loose to make a cup shape. Remove the orange and press the bottom of the foil case gently on a surface to make a flat base. Repeat to make four foil cups.

2 Break half the chocolate into small pieces and place in a bowl set over a pan of very hot water. Stir occasionally until the chocolate has completely melted.

3 Spoon the chocolate into the foil cups, spreading it up the sides with the back of a spoon to give a ragged edge. Chill for 30 minutes in the refrigerator, or until set hard. Gently peel away the foil, starting at the top edge.

4 To make the chocolate mousse, put the remaining chocolate and espresso into a bowl set over a pan of hot water and melt as before, until smooth and liquid. Stir in the butter, a little at a time. Remove the pan from the heat and then stir in the egg yolks.

5 Whisk the egg whites in a bowl until stiff, but not dry, then fold them into the chocolate mixture. Pour into a bowl and chill for at least 3 hours, or until the mousse is set. Scoop the chilled mousse into the chocolate cups just before serving.

Meringue Pyramid with Chocolate Mascarpone

This impressive cake makes a perfect centerpiece for a celebration buffet. Dust the pyramid with a little sifted confectioners' sugar and sprinkle with just a few rose petals for simple, but stunning presentation.

SERVES ABOUT TEN

**7 ounces
semisweet chocolate**

4 egg whites

¾ cup superfine sugar

**½ cup
mascarpone cheese**

COOK'S TIP
The meringues can be made up to a week in advance and stored in a cool, dry place in an airtight container.

1 Preheat the oven to 300°F. Line three large cookie sheets with baking parchment or waxed paper. Grate about 3 ounces of the semisweet chocolate.

2 Whisk the egg whites in a clean, grease-free bowl until they form stiff peaks. Gradually whisk in half the sugar, then add the rest, and whisk until the meringue is very stiff and glossy. Add the grated chocolate and whisk lightly to mix.

3 Draw an 8-inch circle on the lining paper on one of the cookie sheets, turn it upside down, and spread the marked circle evenly with about half the meringue. Spoon the remaining meringue in 28–30 teaspoonfuls on both cookie sheets. Bake the meringue for 1–1½ hours, or until crisp and completely dried out.

4 Make the filling. Melt the remaining chocolate in a heatproof bowl over hot water. Cool slightly, then stir in the mascarpone. Cool the mixture until firm.

5 Spoon the chocolate mixture into a large pastry bag and use to sandwich the meringues together in pairs, reserving a small amount of filling for the pyramid.

6 Arrange the filled meringues on a serving platter, piling them up in a pyramid and keeping them in position with a few well-placed dabs of the reserved filling.

Classic Chocolate Roulade

This rich, squidgy chocolate roll should be made at least eight hours before serving to let it soften. Expect the roulade to crack a little when you roll it up—sprinkle with a little grated chocolate, if you like, as a final decoration. When melting chocolate, break it into even-size pieces and place in a dry, heatproof bowl over hot water. If the water is too hot, the chocolate will turn grainy and scorch; if the chocolate is splashed with water, it will harden and acquire a dull finish.

SERVES EIGHT

1 Preheat the oven to 350°F. Grease and line a 13 x 9 inch jelly roll pan with baking parchment.

2 Break the chocolate into squares and melt in a bowl over a pan of barely simmering water. Remove from the heat and let cool for about 5 minutes.

3 In a large bowl, whisk the sugar and egg yolks until light and fluffy. Stir in the melted chocolate.

4 Whisk the egg whites until stiff, but not dry, and then gently fold into the chocolate mixture.

5 Pour the chocolate mixture into the prepared pan spreading it level with a spatula. Bake for about 25 minutes, or until firm. Leave the cake in the pan and cover with a cooling rack, making sure that it does not touch the cake.

6 Cover the rack with a damp dishtowel, then wrap in plastic wrap. Leave the cake in a cool place for 8 hours, preferably overnight.

7 Dust a sheet of waxed paper with superfine or confectioners' sugar and turn out the roulade onto it. Peel off the lining paper.

8 To make the filling, whip the heavy cream until soft peaks form. Spread the cream over the roulade. Starting from one of the short ends, carefully roll it up, using the paper to help.

9 Place the roulade, seam side down, on a serving plate and dust generously with more superfine or confectioners' sugar before serving.

7 ounces semisweet chocolate

1 cup superfine sugar, plus extra superfine or confectioners' sugar for dusting

7 eggs, separated

1¼ cups heavy cream

COOK'S TIP

For a special dessert, decorate the roulade with swirls of whipped cream and chocolate coffee beans or with clusters of raspberries and mint leaves.

Summer Fruit Brioche

Scooped-out, individual brioches make perfect containers for the fruity filling in this stylish, but simple dessert. If small brioches are not available, serve the fruit on slices cut from a large brioche. Any summer fruits can be used in this dessert—try raspberries, sliced peaches, nectarines, apricots, or pitted cherries. Serve with light cream poured over.

SERVES FOUR

1 Preheat the broiler. Slice the tops off the brioches and use a teaspoon to scoop out their centers, leaving a ½-inch thick case. Lightly toast them, turning once and watching them carefully, as they will brown very quickly.

2 Put the strawberries in a heavy pan with the sugar and add 4 tablespoons water. Heat very gently for about 1 minute, until the strawberries are softened but still keep their shape. Remove the pan from the heat, stir in the raspberries, and let cool.

3 Place the brioches on plates and pile the fruit mixture into them. Add plenty of juice to saturate the brioches and let it flood the plates. Place any extra fruit on the plates.

4 individual brioches

2½ cups small ripe strawberries, halved

2 tablespoons superfine sugar

⅔ cup raspberries

Rhubarb and Ginger Jellies

Made with bright pink, young rhubarb, these softly set jellies get the taste buds tingling. They are spiced with plenty of fresh ginger, which gives just a hint of zesty warmth. Pour the jelly into pretty glasses and serve it as it is or top it with spoonfuls of lightly whipped cream.

SERVES FIVE TO SIX

2¼ pounds young rhubarb

1 cup superfine sugar

2 ounces fresh ginger root, finely chopped

1 tablespoon powdered gelatin

1 Cut the rhubarb into ¾-inch chunks and place in a pan with the sugar and ginger. Pour in scant 2 cups water and bring to a boil. Reduce the heat, cover, and simmer gently for 10 minutes, until the rhubarb is very soft and pulpy.

2 Meanwhile, sprinkle the gelatin over 2 tablespoons cold water in a small heatproof bowl. Let stand, without stirring, for 5 minutes, until the gelatin has become sponge-like in texture. Set the bowl over a small pan of hot water and simmer, stirring occasionally, until the gelatin has dissolved completely into a clear liquid. Remove from the heat.

3 Strain the cooked rhubarb through a fine strainer into a bowl. Stir in the dissolved gelatin until thoroughly mixed. Let cool slightly before pouring into serving glasses. Chill for at least 4 hours or overnight, until set.

Hot Desserts

A HOT DESSERT MAKES THE PERFECT END TO A MEAL
AND CAN TAKE VERY LITTLE TIME TO PREPARE. A FEW
WELL-CHOSEN INGREDIENTS CAN BE TURNED INTO A
SUMPTUOUS, MOUTHWATERING TREAT WITH THE MINIMUM
OF EFFORT. MANY OF THE RECIPES IN THIS CHAPTER CAN
BE PREPARED IN ADVANCE AND SIMPLY POPPED IN THE
OVEN TO COOK WHILE YOU SERVE THE MAIN COURSE.

Broiled Peaches with Meringues

Ripe peaches take on a fabulous scented fruitiness when broiled with brown sugar, and mini meringues are the perfect accompaniment. Serve with crème fraîche flavored with a little grated orange rind. When buying peaches or nectarines, choose fruit with an attractive rosy bloom, avoiding any that have a green-tinged skin or feel hard. Nectarines have a smoother skin than peaches and are actually a type of peach native to China.

SERVES SIX

2 egg whites

½ cup soft light brown sugar, reserving 1 teaspoon for the peaches

pinch of ground cinnamon

6 ripe peaches, or nectarines

1 Preheat the oven to 275°F. Line two large cookie sheets with baking parchment.

2 Whisk the egg whites until they form stiff peaks. Gradually whisk in the sugar and ground cinnamon until the mixture is stiff and glossy. Pipe 18 very small meringues onto the cookie sheets and bake for 40 minutes. Leave in the oven to cool.

3 Meanwhile, halve and pit the peaches or nectarines, sprinkling each half with a little sugar as it is cut. Broil for 4–5 minutes, until just beginning to caramelize.

4 Arrange the broiled peaches on serving plates with the meringues and serve immediately.

COOK'S TIP

Use leftover egg whites to make these little cinnamon-flavored meringues. The meringues can be stored in an airtight container for about 2 weeks. Serve them after dinner with coffee or with desserts in place of cookies.

Summer Berries in Sabayon Glaze

This luxurious combination of summer berries under a light and fluffy liqueur sauce is lightly broiled to form a crisp, caramelized topping. Fresh or frozen berries can be used in this dessert. If you use frozen berries, thaw them in a strainer over a bowl to let the juices drip. Stir a little juice into the fruit before dividing among the dishes.

SERVES FOUR

1 Arrange the mixed summer berries or soft fruit in four individual flameproof dishes. Preheat the broiler.

2 Whisk the egg yolks in a large bowl with the sugar and liqueur or wine. Place over a pan of hot water and whisk constantly until the mixture is thick, fluffy, and pale.

3 Pour equal quantities of the yolk mixture into each dish. Place under the broiler for 1–2 minutes, until just turning brown. Add an extra splash of liqueur, if you like, and serve immediately.

4 cups mixed summer berries, or soft fruit

4 egg yolks

¼ cup vanilla sugar or superfine sugar

½ cup liqueur, such as Cointreau or kirsch, or a white dessert wine

Zabaglione

Light as air and wonderfully heady, this warm, wine egg custard is a much-loved Italian dessert. It is traditionally made with Sicilian Marsala, but other fortified wines such as Madeira or sweet sherry can be used.

SERVES FOUR

1 Place the egg yolks and sugar in a large heatproof bowl and whisk with an electric beater until the mixture is pale and thick.

2 Gradually add the Marsala, Madeira, or sweet sherry to the egg mixture, 1 tablespoon at a time, whisking well after each addition.

3 Place the bowl over a pan of gently simmering water and whisk for 5–7 minutes, until thick: when the beaters are lifted, they should leave a thick trail on the surface of the mixture. Do not be tempted to give up when beating the mixture, as the zabaglione will be too runny and will be likely to separate if it is underbeaten.

4 Pour into four warmed, stemmed glasses and serve immediately, with amaretti for dipping.

4 egg yolks

¼ cup superfine sugar

4 tablespoons Marsala, Madeira, or sweet sherry

amaretti, to serve

EXTRAS
Marinate chopped strawberries in a little extra Marsala, Madeira, or sweet sherry for an hour or so. Sweeten with sugar, if you like, and spoon into the glasses before you add the zabaglione.

Apricot and Ginger Gratin

Made with tangy fresh apricots, this quick and easy dessert has a comforting, baked cheesecake-like flavor. For an even easier version of this delicious gratin, use 14 ounces canned apricots in juice. Use juice from the can to beat into the cream cheese.

SERVES FOUR

1 Put the apricots in a pan with the sugar. Pour in 5 tablespoons water and heat until barely simmering. Cover and cook very gently for 8–10 minutes, until they are tender but still holding their shape.

2 Preheat the oven to 400°F. Drain the apricots, reserving the syrup, and place in a large dish or divide among four individual ovenproof dishes. Set aside 6 tablespoons of the syrup and spoon the remainder over the fruit.

3 Beat the cream cheese until softened, then gradually beat in the reserved syrup until smooth. Spoon the cheese mixture over the apricots. Sprinkle the cookie crumbs over the cream cheese and juice mixture. Bake for 10 minutes, until the crumb topping is beginning to darken and the filling has warmed through. Serve the gratin immediately.

1¼ pounds apricots, halved and pitted

scant ½ cup superfine sugar

scant 1 cup cream cheese

3 ounces gingersnaps, crushed to crumbs

Baked Ricotta Cakes with Red Sauce

These honey-flavored desserts take only minutes to make from a few ingredients. The fragrant fruity sauce provides a contrast of both color and flavor. The red berry sauce can be made a day in advance and chilled until ready to use. Frozen fruit doesn't need extra water, as it usually yields its juice easily on thawing.

SERVES FOUR

generous 1 cup ricotta cheese

2 egg whites, beaten

4 tablespoons scented honey, plus extra to taste

4 cups mixed fresh or frozen fruit, such as strawberries, raspberries, blackberries, and cherries

1 Preheat the oven to 350°F. Place the ricotta cheese in a bowl and break it up with a wooden spoon. Add the beaten egg whites and honey, and mix thoroughly until smooth and well combined.

2 Lightly grease four ramekins. Spoon the ricotta mixture into the prepared ramekins and level the tops. Bake for 20 minutes, or until the ricotta cakes are risen and golden.

3 Meanwhile, make the fruit sauce. Reserve about a fourth of the fruit for decoration. Place the rest of the fruit in a pan, with a little water if the fruit is fresh, and heat gently until softened. Let cool slightly and remove any pits if using cherries.

4 Press the fruit through a strainer, then taste and sweeten with honey if it is too sharp. Serve the sauce, warm or cold, with the ricotta cakes. Decorate with the reserved berries.

Hot Blackberry and Apple Soufflés

The deliciously sharp flavors of blackberry and apple complement each other perfectly to make a light, mouthwatering, and surprisingly low-fat, hot dessert. Running a table knife around the inside edge of the soufflé dishes before baking helps the soufflés to rise evenly without sticking to the rim of the dish. Make this dish in early fall, when there are plentiful supplies of blackberries.

MAKES SIX

1 Preheat the oven to 400°F. Put a cookie sheet in the oven to heat. Cook the blackberries and apple in a pan for 10 minutes, or until the juice runs from the blackberries and the apple has pulped down well. Press through a strainer into a bowl. Stir in ¼ cup superfine sugar. Set aside to cool.

2 Put a spoonful of the fruit purée into each of six ⅔-cup greased and sugared individual soufflé dishes and smooth the surface. Set the dishes aside.

3 Whisk the egg whites in a large bowl until they form stiff peaks. Gradually whisk in the remaining superfine sugar. Fold in the remaining fruit purée and spoon the flavored meringue into the prepared dishes. Level the tops with a metal spatula and run a table knife around the edge of each dish.

4 Place the dishes on the hot cookie sheet and bake for 10–15 minutes, until the soufflés have risen well and are lightly browned. Dust the tops with a little sugar and serve immediately.

3 cups blackberries

1 large cooking apple, peeled and finely diced

3 egg whites

¼ cup superfine sugar, plus extra superfine or confectioners' sugar for dusting

Warm Chocolate Zabaglione

Once you've tasted this sensuous dessert, you'll never regard cocoa in quite the same way again. The dark zabaglione can be dusted with confectioners' sugar instead of extra cocoa, if you like. Serve with mini amaretti or other small, crisp cookies.

SERVES SIX

6 egg yolks

¾ cup superfine sugar

3 tablespoons unsweetened cocoa powder, plus extra for dusting

scant 1 cup Marsala

1 Prepare a pan of simmering water and a heatproof bowl to fit on top. Place the egg yolks and sugar in the bowl and whisk, off the heat, until the mixture is pale and all the sugar has dissolved.

2 Add the cocoa and Marsala, then place the bowl over the simmering water. Beat with a hand-held electric mixer until the mixture is smooth, thick and foamy.

3 Pour quickly into tall glasses, dust lightly with cocoa, and serve immediately, with amaretti or other dessert cookies, if liked.

Hot Chocolate Rum Soufflés

Light as air, melt-in-the-mouth soufflés are always impressive, yet they are often based on the simplest pantry ingredients. Serve them as soon as they are cooked for a fantastic finale to a special dinner party. For an extra indulgent touch, serve the soufflés with whipped cream flavored with dark rum and finely grated orange rind.

SERVES SIX

½ cup unsweetened
cocoa powder

5 tablespoons
superfine sugar, plus
extra superfine or
confectioners' sugar
for dusting

2 tablespoons dark rum

6 egg whites

1 Preheat the oven to 375°F. Place a cookie sheet in the oven to heat up.

2 Mix 1 tablespoon of the unsweetened cocoa powder with 1 tablespoon of the sugar in a bowl. Grease six 1-cup ramekins. Pour the cocoa and sugar mixture into each of the dishes in turn, rotating them so that they are evenly coated.

3 Mix the remaining unsweetened cocoa powder with the dark rum in a bowl.

4 Whisk the egg whites in a clean, grease-free bowl until they form stiff peaks. Whisk in the remaining sugar. Stir a generous spoonful of the whites into the cocoa mixture to lighten it, then fold in the remaining whites.

5 Divide the mixture among the dishes. Place on the hot cookie sheet, and bake for 13–15 minutes, or until well risen. Dust with superfine or confectioners' sugar before serving.

COOK'S TIP

When serving the soufflés at the end of a dinner party, prepare them just before the meal is served. Put them in the oven when the main course is finished and serve steaming hot.

Caramelized Upside-down Pear Pie

In this gloriously sticky dessert, which is almost like the French classic *tarte tatin*, the pastry is baked on top of the fruit, which gives it a crisp and flaky texture. When inverted, the pie looks wonderful. Look for good-quality chilled pastry that you can freeze for future use. Serve with whipped cream, ice cream, or just plain for a gloriously sticky dessert.

SERVES EIGHT

1 Peel the pears, cut into fourths, and core. Toss with some of the sugar in a bowl.

2 Melt the butter in a 10½-inch heavy, ovenproof omelet pan. Add the remaining sugar. When it changes color, arrange the pears in the pan.

3 Continue cooking, uncovered, for 20 minutes, or until the fruit has completely caramelized.

4 Let the fruit cool in the pan. Preheat the oven to 400°F. Meanwhile, on a lightly floured surface, roll out the pastry to a round that is slightly larger than the diameter of the pan. Lay the pastry on top of the pears and then carefully tuck it in around the edge.

5 Bake for 15 minutes, then lower the oven temperature to 350°F. Bake for 15 minutes more, or until the pastry is golden.

6 Let the pie cool in the pan for a few minutes. To unmold, run a knife around the pan's edge, then, using potholders, invert a plate over the pan, and quickly turn the two over together.

7 If any pears stick to the pan, remove them gently with a metal spatula and replace them on the pie. The pie is best served warm.

5–6 firm, ripe pears

scant 1 cup superfine sugar

½ cup butter

8 ounces unsweetened shortcrust pastry dough

VARIATIONS

• To make caramelized upside-down apple pie, replace the pears with eight or nine firm, full-flavored eating apples— Cox's Orange Pippins would be a good choice. You will need more apples than pears, as they shrink during cooking.

• Nectarines or peaches also work well, as does rhubarb. Rhubarb is sharp, so you may need to add more sugar.

Peach Pie

Fruit pies do not have to be restricted to the chunky, deep-dish variety. Here, juicy, ripe peaches are encased in crisp pastry to make a glorious puffed dome—simple but delicious. For a really crispy crust, glaze the pie with beaten egg yolk thinned with a little water before sprinkling with sugar. Serve the pie with good quality vanilla ice cream or thick cream.

SERVES EIGHT

1 Blanch the peaches for 30 seconds. Drain, refresh in cold water, then peel. Halve, pit, and slice the peaches.

2 Melt the butter in a large skillet. Add the peach slices, then sprinkle with 1 tablespoon water and the sugar. Cook for about 4 minutes, shaking the skillet frequently, or until the sugar has dissolved and the peaches are tender. Set the pan aside to cool.

3 Cut the pastry into two pieces, one slightly larger than the other. Roll out on a lightly floured surface and, using plates as a guide, cut a 12-inch round and an 11-inch round. Place the pastry rounds on cookie sheets lined with baking parchment, cover with plastic wrap, and chill for 30 minutes.

4 Preheat the oven to 400°F. Remove the plastic wrap from the pastry rounds. Spoon the peaches into the middle of the larger round and spread them out to within 2 inches of the edge. Place the smaller pastry round on top. Brush the edge of the larger pastry round with water, then fold this over the top round, and press to seal. Twist the edges together to seal.

5 Lightly brush the pastry with water and sprinkle evenly with a little sugar. Make five or six small crescent-shape slashes on the top of the pastry. Bake the pie for about 45 minutes and serve warm.

6 large, firm ripe peaches

3 tablespoons butter

6 tablespoons superfine sugar, plus extra for glazing

1 pound puff pastry dough

EXTRAS *Brandy, peach liqueur, or peach schnapps would be superb with the peaches in this pie: add 3 tablespoons instead of the water in step 2.*

Treacle Tart

The best chilled commercial shortcrust pastry makes light work of this old-fashioned favorite, with its sticky filling and twisted lattice topping. Smooth creamy custard is the classic accompaniment, but it is also delicious served with cream or ice cream. For a more textured filling, use whole-wheat bread crumbs or crushed cornflakes instead of the white bread crumbs.

SERVES FOUR TO SIX

1 On a lightly floured surface, roll out three-fourths of the pastry to a thickness of ⅛ inch. Transfer to an 8-inch fluted quiche pan and trim off the overhang. Chill the pie shell for 20 minutes. Reserve the pastry trimmings.

2 Put a cookie sheet in the oven and preheat to 400°F. To make the filling, warm the syrup in a pan until it melts. Grate the lemon rind and squeeze the juice.

3 Remove the syrup from the heat and stir in the bread crumbs and lemon rind. Let stand for 10 minutes, then add more crumbs if the mixture is too thin and moist. Stir in 2 tablespoons of the lemon juice, then spread the mixture evenly in the pie shell.

4 Roll out the reserved pastry and cut into 10–12 thin strips. Twist the strips into spirals, then lay half of them on the filling. Arrange the remaining strips at right angles to form a lattice. Press the ends onto the rim.

5 Place the tart on the hot cookie sheet and bake for 10 minutes. Lower the oven temperature to 375°F. Bake for 15 minutes more, until golden. Serve warm.

12 ounces unsweetened shortcrust pastry

generous ¾ cup light corn syrup

1 lemon

1½ cups fresh white bread crumbs

Blueberry and Almond Tart

This is a cheat's version of a sweet almond tart and the result is superb. Whisked egg whites and grated marzipan cook to form a light sponge under a tangy topping of contrasting blueberries. When whisking the egg whites for the filling, make sure all traces of yolk are removed—otherwise you won't be able to whisk them to their maximum volume.

SERVES SIX

9 ounces unsweetened shortcrust pastry

generous 1 cup white marzipan

4 extra large egg whites

generous 1 cup blueberries

1 Preheat the oven to 400°F. Roll out the pastry and use to line a 9-inch round, loose-based quiche pan. Line with waxed paper and fill with baking beans, then bake for 15 minutes. Remove the beans and waxed paper and bake for 5 minutes more. Reduce the oven temperature to 350°F.

2 Grate the marzipan. Whisk the egg whites until stiff. Sprinkle half the marzipan over them and fold in. Then fold in the rest.

3 Turn the mixture into the pie shell and spread it evenly. Sprinkle the blueberries over the top and bake for 20–25 minutes, until golden and just set. Let cool for 10 minutes before serving.

Baked Bananas with Ice Cream and Toffee Sauce

Bananas make one of the easiest of all desserts, just as welcome as a comforting winter treat as they are to follow a barbecue. For an extra sweet finishing touch, grate some semisweet chocolate on the bananas, over the sauce, just before serving. If baking on a barbecue, turn the bananas occasionally to insure even cooking.

SERVES FOUR

4 large bananas

scant ½ cup light brown sugar

5 tablespoons heavy cream

4 scoops good-quality vanilla ice cream

1 Preheat the oven to 350°F. Put the unpeeled bananas in an ovenproof dish and bake for 15–20 minutes, until the skins are very dark and the flesh feels soft when squeezed.

2 Meanwhile, heat the light molasses sugar in a small, heavy pan with 5 tablespoons water until dissolved. Bring to a boil and add the heavy cream. Cook for 5 minutes, until the sauce has thickened and is toffee colored. Remove from the heat.

3 Transfer the baked bananas in their skins to serving plates and split them lengthwise to reveal the flesh. Pour some of the sauce over the bananas and top with scoops of vanilla ice cream. Serve any remaining sauce separately.

Cakes, Cookies and Candies

HOME-BAKED CAKES AND SWEET SNACKS ARE THE
ULTIMATE INDULGENCE BUT ARE VIEWED BY MANY AS
TAKING TOO MUCH TIME AND EFFORT. HOWEVER, WITH
JUST A FEW BASIC INGREDIENTS, YOU CAN WHIP UP
FABULOUS CAKES, COOKIES AND CANDIES IN MOMENTS.
TRY DELICIOUS TREATS SUCH AS CHOCOLATE BROWNIES,
CHEWY FLAPJACKS OR QUICK AND EASY TEABREAD.

Chewy Flapjacks

Flapjacks are popular with adults and children alike and they are so quick and easy to make. For alternative versions of the basic recipe, stir in ¼ cup finely chopped ready-to-eat dried apricots or golden raisins. To make a really decadent treat, you can dip the cooled flapjack fingers into melted chocolate, to half cover.

MAKES TWELVE

1 Preheat the oven to 350°F. Line the base and sides of an 8-inch square cake pan with baking parchment.

2 Combine the butter, sugar, and syrup in a pan and heat gently until the butter has melted. Add the oats and stir until all the ingredients are combined. Turn the mixture into the pan and level the surface.

3 Bake the flapjacks for 15–20 minutes, until just beginning to turn golden. Let cool slightly, then cut into bars, and remove from the pan. Store in an airtight container.

¼ cup sweet butter

¼ cup superfine sugar

scant ⅔ cup light corn syrup

1½ cups rolled oats

Quick and Easy Teabread

This succulent, fruity teabread can be served just as it is, or spread with a little butter. The loaf can be stored, tightly wrapped in foil or in an airtight container, for up to five days. A great way to get children to eat some fruit, this teabread is ideal for school lunches, picnics, or simply served with a glass of milk for an after-school snack.

SERVES EIGHT

1 Put the fruit in a bowl. Add ⅔ cup boiling water and let stand for 30 minutes.

2 Preheat the oven to 350°F. Grease and line the base and long sides of a 1-pound loaf pan.

3 Beat the main quantity of sugar and the egg into the fruit. Sift the flour into the bowl and stir until combined. Turn into the prepared pan and level the surface. Sprinkle with the remaining sugar.

4 Bake the bread for about 50 minutes, until risen and firm to the touch. When it is cooked, a skewer inserted into the center will come out without any sticky mixture on it. Leave the loaf in the pan for 10 minutes before turning out onto a wire rack to cool.

2 cups luxury mixed dried fruit

scant ⅓ cup raw sugar, plus 1 tablespoon

1 extra large egg

1½ cups self-rising flour

Orange and Pecan Biscuits

Serve these nutty orange biscuits with satiny orange or lemon curd or, for a simple, unsweetened snack, fresh and warm with sweet butter. Biscuits are best served on the day they are made, or they can be frozen. To freeze, place in an airtight container. To thaw, remove from the freezer and thaw at room temperature for an hour.

MAKES TEN

1 Preheat the oven to 425°F. Grease a cookie sheet. Put the flour in a food processor with a pinch of salt and add the butter. Process the mixture until it resembles coarse bread crumbs.

2 Add the orange rind. Reserve 2 tablespoons of the orange juice and make the remainder up to 1½ cups with water. Add the nuts and the juice mixture to the processor, process very briefly to a firm dough, adding a little water if the dough feels dry.

3 Turn the dough out onto a lightly floured surface and roll out to ¾ inch thick. Cut out biscuits using a round cutter and transfer them to the cookie sheet. Re-roll the trimmings and cut more biscuits. Brush the biscuits with the reserved juice and bake for 15–20 minutes, until golden. Transfer to a wire rack to cool.

2 cups self-rising flour

¼ cup sweet butter, chilled and diced

grated rind and juice of 1 orange

1 cup pecan nuts, coarsely chopped

Creamed Coconut Macaroons

Finely grated creamed coconut gives these soft-centered cookies a rich creaminess. Cooking the gooey mixture on baking parchment makes sure that the cookies are easily removed from the cookie sheet. For a tangy flavor, add the grated rind of one lime to the mixture in step 2. The cooked macaroons can be stored in an airtight container for up to one week.

MAKES SIXTEEN TO EIGHTEEN

1 Preheat the oven to 350°F. Line a large cookie sheet with baking parchment. Finely grate the creamed coconut.

2 Use an electric beater to whisk the egg whites in a large bowl until stiff. Whisk in the sugar, a little at a time, to make a stiff and glossy meringue. Fold in the grated creamed and dry unsweetened shredded coconut, using a large, metal spoon.

3 Place dessertspoonfuls of the mixture, spaced slightly apart, on the cookie sheet. Bake for 15–20 minutes, until slightly risen and golden brown. Let cool on the parchment, then transfer to an airtight container.

1 cup creamed coconut, chilled

2 extra large egg whites

½ cup superfine sugar

1 cup dry unsweetened shredded coconut

Rich Chocolate Brownies

These brownies are packed with both milk and dark chocolate instead of adding sugar to the mixture. Serve them in small squares as they are very rich. When buying semisweet chocolate, bear in mind that the higher the percentage of cocoa solids, the higher the quality of the chocolate, and the less sugar it contains. The best quality has 70 percent cocoa solids.

MAKES SIXTEEN

1 Preheat the oven to 350°F. Line the base and sides of an 8-inch square cake pan with baking parchment.

2 Break the semisweet chocolate and 3½ ounces of the milk chocolate into pieces and put in a heatproof bowl with the butter. Melt over a pan of barely simmering water, stirring frequently.

3 Chop the remaining milk chocolate into chunky pieces. Stir the flour and eggs into the melted chocolate until evenly combined. Stir in half the chopped milk chocolate and turn the mixture into the prepared pan, spreading it into the corners. Sprinkle with the remaining chopped chocolate.

4 Bake the brownies for 30–35 minutes, until risen and just firm to the touch. Let cool in the pan, then cut the mixture into squares. Store the brownies in an airtight container.

12 ounces each semisweet and milk chocolate

¼ cup sweet butter

⅔ cup self-rising flour

3 extra large eggs

Rich Chocolate Cookie Slice

This dark chocolate refrigerator cake is packed with crisp cookie pieces and chunks of white chocolate for color and flavor contrast. The slice is perfect served with strong coffee, either as a morning treat or in place of dessert. Once set, cut the cake into slices and store the slices in an airtight container in the refrigerator until ready to serve.

SERVES EIGHT TO TEN

**10 ounces
fruit and nut
semisweet chocolate**

**9 tablespoons
sweet butter**

**3½ ounces
graham crackers**

**3½ ounces
white chocolate**

1 Grease and line the base and sides of a 1-pound loaf pan with baking parchment. Break the fruit and nut chocolate into pieces and place in a heatproof bowl with the butter. Place the bowl over a pan of barely simmering water and stir the chocolate gently until it is melted and smooth. Remove the bowl from the pan and let cool for 20 minutes.

2 Break the cookies into small pieces. Finely chop the white chocolate. Stir the cookies and white chocolate into the melted mixture until evenly combined. Turn the mixture into the prepared pan and pack down gently. Chill for about 2 hours, or until set. Cut the mixture into slices.

Cinnamon Pinwheels

These impressive sweet pastries go well with tea or coffee or as an accompaniment to ice cream and creamy desserts. If you find they turn soft during storage, re-crisp them briefly in the oven. Cinnamon is widely used in both sweet and savory cookery: here, ground cinnamon is used but it is also available as woody sticks. It has a delicious fragrant aroma and gives these simple-to-make pinwheels a warm spicy flavor.

MAKES TWENTY TO TWENTY-FOUR

¼ cup superfine sugar, plus a little extra for sprinkling

2 teaspoons ground cinnamon

9 ounces puff pastry dough

beaten egg, to glaze

1 Preheat the oven to 425°F. Grease a large cookie sheet. Mix the sugar with the cinnamon in a small bowl.

2 Roll out the pastry on a lightly floured surface to an 8-inch square and sprinkle with half the sugar mixture. Roll out the pastry to a 10-inch square so that the sugar is pressed into it.

3 Brush with the beaten egg and then sprinkle with the remaining sugar mixture. Loosely roll up the pastry into a log, brushing the end of the pastry with a little more egg to secure the edge in place.

4 Using a sharp knife, cut the log into thin slices and transfer them to the prepared cookie sheet. Bake for 10 minutes, until golden and crisp. Sprinkle with more sugar and transfer to a wire rack to cool.

Almond Cigars

These simple, Moroccan-inspired pastries can be prepared in minutes. They are perfect served with strong black coffee or as an after-dinner treat. They are also delicious served with traditional sweet Moroccan mint tea. To serve, the pastries look very pretty sprinkled with a little confectioners' sugar as a simple finishing touch.

MAKES EIGHT TO TWELVE

9 ounces marzipan

1 egg, lightly beaten

8–12 sheets phyllo pastry

melted butter, for brushing

1 Knead the marzipan until soft and pliable, then put it in a mixing bowl, and mix in the lightly beaten egg. Chill in the refrigerator for 1–2 hours.

2 Preheat the oven to 375°F. Lightly grease a cookie sheet. Place a sheet of phyllo pastry on a piece of waxed paper, keeping the remaining pastry covered with a damp cloth, and brush with the melted butter.

3 Shape 2–3 tablespoons of the almond paste into a cylinder and place at one end of the pastry. Fold the pastry over to enclose the ends of the paste, then roll up to form a cigar shape. Place on the cookie sheet and make 7–11 more cigars in the same way.

4 Bake the pastries in the preheated oven for about 15 minutes, or until golden brown in color. Transfer to a wire rack to cool before serving.

All Butter Cookies

Crisp, buttery cookies are perfect with strawberries and cream or any creamy dessert or fruit compote. These cookies are known as refrigerator cookies as the mixture is chilled until it is firm enough to cut neatly into thin cookies. The dough can be frozen and when thawed enough to slice, can be freshly baked, but do allow a little extra cooking time.

MAKES TWENTY-EIGHT TO THIRTY

1 Put the flour in a food processor. Add the butter and process until the mixture resembles coarse bread crumbs. Add the confectioners' sugar and vanilla, and process until the mixture comes together to form a dough. Knead lightly and shape into a thick sausage, 12 inches long and 2 inches in diameter. Wrap and chill for at least 1 hour, until firm.

2 Preheat the oven to 400°F. Grease two cookie sheets. Using a sharp knife, cut ¼-inch thick slices from the dough and space them slightly apart on the cookie sheet.

3 Bake for 8–10 minutes, alternating the position of the cookie sheets in the oven halfway through cooking, if necessary, until the cookies are cooked evenly and have just turned pale golden around the edges. Leave for 5 minutes, then transfer to a wire rack to cool. Serve dusted with confectioners' sugar.

2½ cups all-purpose flour

scant 1 cup sweet butter

scant 1 cup confectioners' sugar, plus extra for dusting

2 teaspoons vanilla extract

Almond Cookies

These short, light cookies have a melt-in-the-mouth texture. Their simplicity means they are endlessly versatile—irresistible with tea or coffee and stylish with special desserts.

MAKES ABOUT TWENTY-FOUR

1 cup all-purpose flour

1½ cups confectioners' sugar, plus extra for dusting

½ cup chopped almonds, plus halved almonds to decorate

½ cup sweet butter, softened

1 Preheat the oven to 350°F. Combine the flour, sugar, and chopped almonds in a bowl.

2 Put the softened sweet butter in the center of the flour and nut mixture and use a blunt knife or your fingertips to draw the dry ingredients into the butter until a dough is formed. Shape the dough into a ball.

3 Place the dough on a lightly floured surface and roll it out to a thickness of about ⅛ inch. Using a 3-inch cookie cutter, cut out about 24 rounds, re-rolling the dough as necessary. Place the dough rounds on cookie sheets, leaving a little space between them. Bake the cookies for 25–30 minutes, until pale golden.

4 Leave the cooked cookies on the cookie sheet for 10 minutes, then transfer to wire racks to cool. Dust thickly with sifted confectioners' sugar before serving, decorated with halved almonds.

COOK'S TIP

Use fancy cutters to make these cookies look even more interesting. Hearts, stars, and crescents are three shapes that you might like to try.

Golden Ginger Macaroons

Macaroons are classic no-fuss cookies—easy to whisk up in minutes from the minimum ingredients and always acceptable. A hint of ginger makes this recipe that bit different. For a darker color and slightly richer flavor, use soft dark brown sugar instead. Bake these cookies on nonstick cookie sheets or on a cookie sheet lined with baking parchment to prevent them from sticking.

MAKES EIGHTEEN TO TWENTY

1 Preheat the oven to 350°F. In a large, grease-free bowl, whisk the egg white until stiff and standing in peaks, but not dry and crumbly, then whisk in the brown sugar.

2 Sprinkle the ground almonds and ginger over the whisked egg white and gently fold them together.

3 Using two teaspoons, place spoonfuls of the mixture on cookie sheets, leaving plenty of space between each. Bake for about 20 minutes, until pale golden brown and just turning crisp.

4 Let cool slightly on the cookie sheets before transferring to a wire rack to cool completely.

1 egg white

scant ½ cup soft light brown sugar

1 cup ground almonds

1 teaspoon ground ginger

VARIATION *Other ground nuts, such as hazelnuts or walnuts, are good alternatives to the almonds. Ground cinnamon or apple pie spice can be used instead of the ginger for a mellower flavor.*

Nutty Nougat

Nougat is an almost magical sweetmeat that emerges from honey-flavored meringue made with boiled syrup. Since any other nuts or candied fruits can be used instead of almonds, as long as you have eggs, sugar, and honey, you have the potential for making an impromptu gift or dinner-party treat.

MAKES ABOUT 1¼ POUNDS

1 Line a 7-inch square cake pan with rice paper. Place the granulated sugar, honey or syrup, and 4 tablespoons water in a large, heavy pan and heat gently, stirring frequently, until the sugar has completely dissolved.

2 Bring the syrup to a boil and boil gently to the soft crack stage (when the syrup dropped into cold water separates into hard but not brittle threads) or 304°F on a sugar thermometer.

3 Meanwhile, whisk the egg white until very stiff, but not crumbly, then slowly drizzle in the syrup while whisking constantly.

4 Quickly stir in the nuts and pour the mixture into the prepared pan. Let cool but before the nougat becomes too hard, cut it into squares. Store in an airtight container.

generous 1 cup granulated sugar

1 cup honey or light corn syrup

1 extra large egg white

1 cup sliced almonds or chopped pistachio nuts, roasted

Stuffed Prunes

Prunes and semisweet chocolate are delectable partners, especially when the dried fruit is soaked in Armagnac. Serve these sophisticated sweetmeats dusted with unsweetened cocoa powder as a treat with coffee.

MAKES ABOUT THIRTY

1 Put the prunes in a bowl and pour the Armagnac over. Stir, then cover with plastic wrap, and set aside for 2 hours, or until the prunes have absorbed the liquid.

2 Make a slit along each prune to remove the pit, making a hollow for the filling, but leaving the fruit intact.

3 Heat the cream in a pan almost to boiling point. Put 4 ounces of the chocolate in a bowl and pour over the hot cream.

4 Stir until the chocolate has melted and the mixture is smooth. Let cool, until it has the consistency of softened butter.

5 Fill a pastry bag with a small plain tip with the chocolate mixture. Pipe into the cavities of the prunes. Chill for about 20 minutes.

6 Melt the remaining chocolate in a heatproof bowl set over a pan of barely simmering water. Using a fork, dip the prunes, one at a time, into the chocolate to coat them generously. Place on baking parchment to set.

1 cup unpitted prunes

¼ cup Armagnac

⅔ cup heavy cream

12 ounces semisweet chocolate, broken into squares

COOK'S TIP

Armagnac is a type of French brandy produced in the Pay de Gascogne in the southwest of the country. It has a pale color and a cookie-like aroma. Other types of brandy can be used in this recipe.

Chocolate Truffles

Luxurious truffles are expensive to buy but very easy and fun to make. These rich melt-in-the-mouth treats are flavored with coffee liqueur, but you could use whiskey or brandy instead. The mixture can be rolled in unsweetened cocoa powder or confectioners' sugar instead of being dipped in melted chocolate. Remember to store the fresh-cream truffles in the refrigerator.

MAKES TWENTY-FOUR

1 Melt 8 ounces of the semisweet chocolate in a heatproof bowl set over a pan of barely simmering water. Stir in the cream and liqueur, then chill the mixture for 4 hours, until firm.

2 Divide the mixture into 24 equal pieces and quickly roll each into a ball. Chill for about 1 hour, or until the truffles are firm again.

3 Melt the remaining semisweet and the white or milk chocolate in separate small bowls. Using two forks, carefully dip eight of the truffles, one at a time, into the melted semisweet chocolate.

4 Repeat to cover the remaining 16 truffles with the melted white or milk chocolate. Place the truffles on a board or tray, covered with waxed paper or foil. Let set before placing in individual mini paper cases or transferring to a serving dish.

12 ounces semisweet chocolate

5 tablespoons heavy cream

2 tablespoons coffee liqueur, such as Tia Maria, Kahlúa, or Toussaint

8 ounces good-quality white or milk dessert chocolate

EXTRAS

Ring the changes by adding one of the following to the mixture:

GINGER
Stir in ¼ cup finely chopped crystallized ginger.

CANDIED FRUIT
Stir in ⅓ cup finely chopped candied fruit, such as pineapple and orange.

PISTACHIOS
Stir in ¼ cup chopped skinned pistachio nuts.

HAZELNUTS
Roll each ball of chilled truffle mixture around a whole skinned hazelnut.

Breads

THERE ARE FEW FOODS SO DELICIOUS AND COMFORTING
AS FRESHLY BAKED BREAD. THREE BASIC INGREDIENTS —
FLOUR, SALT AND YEAST MIXED WITH WATER ARE ALL THAT
IS NEEDED TO MAKE A BASIC LOAF, WHILE THE ADDITION
OF A FOURTH INGREDIENT SUCH AS HERBS, SUN-DRIED
TOMATOES, OLIVE OIL OR MILK CAN CREATE
WONDERFUL, ENTICING VARIATIONS.

Multigrain Cob

Mixing and shaping a simple round loaf is one of the most satisfying kitchen activities and the result is incomparably excellent. This bread is made with fresh yeast—it is a similar color and texture to putty and should crumble easily when broken. For best results, buy fresh yeast in small quantities as required: it will keep for up to one month in the refrigerator.

MAKES ONE ROUND LOAF

4 cups multigrain or malthouse flour

2½ teaspoons salt

½ ounce fresh yeast

wheat flakes or cracked wheat, for sprinkling

1 Lightly flour a cookie sheet. Combine the flour and 2 teaspoons of the salt in a large bowl and make a well in the center. Place in a very low oven for 5 minutes to warm.

2 Measure 1¼ cups lukewarm water. Mix the yeast with a little of the water, then blend in the rest. Pour the yeast mixture into the center of the flour and mix to a dough.

3 Turn out onto a lightly floured surface and knead for about 10 minutes, until smooth and elastic. Place in a lightly oiled bowl, cover with lightly oiled plastic wrap, and leave to rise in a warm place for 1¼ hours, or until doubled in bulk.

4 Turn the dough out onto a lightly floured surface and punch down. Knead for 2–3 minutes, then roll into a ball. Place in the center of the prepared cookie sheet. Cover with an inverted bowl and leave to rise in a warm place for 30–45 minutes.

5 Preheat the oven to 450°F toward the end of the rising time. Mix 2 tablespoons water with the remaining salt and brush evenly over the bread. Sprinkle the loaf evenly with wheat flakes or cracked wheat.

6 Bake the bread for 15 minutes, then reduce the oven temperature to 400°F and bake for 20 minutes more, or until the loaf is firm to the touch and sounds hollow when tapped on the base. Cool on a wire rack.

Grant Loaves

This quick and easy recipe was created by a baker called Doris Grant and was published in the 1940s. It is a dream for busy cooks as the dough requires no kneading and takes only a minute to mix. Nowadays, we can make the recipe even quicker by using rapid-rise yeast, which is added directly to the dry ingredients.

MAKES THREE LOAVES

1 Thoroughly grease three loaf pans, each 8½ x 4½ x 2½ inches and set aside in a warm place. Sift the flour and salt together in a large bowl and warm slightly to take off the chill.

2 Sprinkle the dried yeast over 1⅔ cups lukewarm water. After a couple of minutes, stir in the molasses sugar. Leave the mixture for 10 minutes.

3 Make a well in the center of the flour. Pour in the yeast mixture and add a further 3¾ cups lukewarm water. Stir to form a slippery dough. Mix for about 1 minute, working the dry ingredients from the sides into the middle.

4 Divide among the prepared pans, cover with oiled plastic wrap, and leave to rise in a warm place for about 30 minutes, or until the dough has risen by about a third to within about ½ inch of the top of the pans.

5 Meanwhile, preheat the oven to 400°F. Bake for 40 minutes, or until the loaves are crisp and sound hollow when tapped on the base. Turn out onto a wire rack to cool.

12 cups whole-wheat bread flour

1 tablespoon salt

1 tablespoon rapid-rise dried yeast

1 tablespoon molasses sugar

Cottage Loaf

Create a culinary masterpiece from a few basic ingredients and experience the satisfaction of traditional baking. Serve this classic-shaped loaf to accompany homemade soup.

MAKES ONE LARGE ROUND LOAF

**6 cups unbleached
strong white
bread flour**

2 teaspoons salt

¾ ounce fresh yeast

1 Lightly grease two cookie sheets. Sift the flour and salt together into a large bowl and make a well in the center.

2 Mix the yeast in ⅔ cup lukewarm water until dissolved. Pour into the center of the flour and add a further 1 cup lukewarm water, then mix to a firm dough.

3 Knead the dough on a lightly floured surface for 10 minutes, until it is smooth and elastic. Place in a lightly oiled bowl, cover with lightly oiled plastic wrap, and leave to rise in a warm place for about 1 hour.

4 Turn out onto a lightly floured surface and punch down. Knead for 2–3 minutes, then divide the dough into two-thirds and one-third, and shape each piece into a ball. Place the balls of dough on the prepared cookie sheets. Cover with inverted bowls and leave to rise in a warm place for 30 minutes.

5 Gently flatten the top of the larger round of dough and cut a cross in the center, about 1½ inches across. Brush with a little water and place the smaller round on top. Carefully press a hole through the middle of the top ball, down into the lower part, using your thumb and first two fingers. Cover with lightly oiled plastic wrap and leave to rest in a warm place for about 10 minutes.

6 Preheat the oven to 425°F and place the bread on the lower shelf of the oven. Bake for 35–40 minutes, or until a rich golden brown color. Cool on a wire rack before serving.

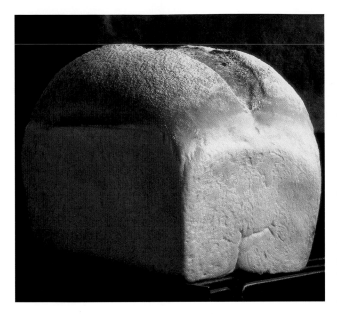

Split Pan

The deep center split down this loaf gives it its name. The split pan loaf slices well for making thick-cut sandwiches, or for serving hearty chunks of bread to accompany robust cheese.

MAKES ONE LOAF

5 cups unbleached strong white bread flour, plus extra for dusting

2 teaspoons salt

½ ounce fresh yeast

4 tablespoons lukewarm milk

1 Grease a 2-pound loaf pan. Sift the flour and salt into a bowl and make a well in the center. Mix the yeast with ⅔ cup lukewarm water. Stir in another ⅔ cup lukewarm water. Pour the yeast mixture into the center of the flour and using your fingers, mix in a little flour to form a smooth batter.

2 Sprinkle a little more flour from around the edge over the batter and leave in a warm place for about 20 minutes to "sponge." Add the milk and remaining flour; mix to a firm dough.

3 Place on a lightly floured surface and knead for about 10 minutes, until smooth and elastic. Place in a lightly oiled bowl, cover with lightly oiled plastic wrap, and leave to rise in a warm place for 1–1¼ hours, or until nearly doubled in bulk.

4 Punch down the dough and turn out onto a lightly floured surface. Shape it into a rectangle, the length of the prepared pan. Roll the dough up lengthwise, tuck the ends under, and place, seam side down, in the pan. Cover the loaf and leave to rise in a warm place for about 20–30 minutes.

5 Using a sharp knife, make one deep central slash. Dust the top of the loaf with a little sifted flour. Leave for 10–15 minutes. Meanwhile, preheat the oven to 450°F. Bake the loaf for 15 minutes, then reduce the oven temperature to 400°F. Bake for 20–25 minutes, until golden and it sounds hollow when tapped on the base. Cool on a wire rack.

Poppy-seeded Bloomer

This long, crusty loaf gets its fabulous flavor from poppy seeds. Cut into thick slices, the bread is perfect for mopping up the cooking juices of hearty stews, or for absorbing good dressing on summery salads. A variety of seeds can be used to add flavor, texture, and color to this loaf—try sunflower, pumpkin, or sesame seeds as an alternative to the poppy seeds. Brushing the loaf with the salted water before baking helps to give it a crisp, crusty finish.

MAKES ONE LARGE LOAF

1 Lightly grease a cookie sheet. Sift the flour and 2 teaspoons of the salt together into a large bowl and make a well in the center.

2 Measure scant 2 cups lukewarm water and stir about a third of it into the yeast in a bowl. Stir in the remaining water and pour into the center of the flour. Mix, gradually incorporating the surrounding flour, to a firm dough.

3 Turn out onto a lightly floured surface and knead the dough very well for at least 10 minutes, until smooth and elastic. Place the dough in a lightly oiled bowl, cover with lightly oiled plastic wrap, and leave to rise, at cool room temperature (about 160–65°F), for 5–6 hours, or until doubled in bulk.

4 Punch down the dough, turn out onto a lightly floured surface, and knead it thoroughly for about 5 minutes. Return the dough to the bowl and re-cover. Leave to rise, at cool room temperature, for 2 hours or slightly longer.

5 Punch down again and repeat the thorough kneading. Leave the dough to rest for 5 minutes, then roll out on a lightly floured surface into a rectangle 1 inch thick. Roll the dough up from one long side and shape it into a square-ended, thick baton shape about 13 x 5 inches.

6 Place the loaf, seam side up, on a lightly floured cookie sheet. Cover with lightly oiled plastic wrap and leave to rest for 15 minutes. Turn the loaf over and place on the greased cookie sheet. Plump the loaf up by tucking the dough under the sides and ends. Using a sharp knife, cut six diagonal slashes on the top.

7 Leave the loaf to rest, covered, in a warm place, for 10 minutes. Meanwhile, preheat the oven to 450°F.

8 Mix the remaining salt with 2 tablespoons water and brush this glaze over the bread. Sprinkle with poppy seeds.

9 Spray the oven with water, bake the bread immediately for 20 minutes, then reduce the oven temperature to 400°F. Bake for 25 minutes more, or until golden and it sounds hollow when tapped on the base. Transfer to a wire rack to cool.

6 cups unbleached strong white bread flour

2½ teaspoons salt

½ ounce fresh yeast

poppy seeds, for sprinkling

COOK'S TIP

The traditional cracked, crusty appearance of this loaf is difficult to achieve in a domestic oven. However, you can get a similar result by spraying the oven with water before baking. If the underneath of the loaf is not very crusty at the end of baking, turn it over on the cookie sheet, switch off the heat, and leave it in the oven for 5–10 minutes more.

French Baguette

Fine French flour is available from French delicatessens and superior supermarkets. If you cannot find any, try ordinary all-purpose flour instead. Baguettes have a wide variety of uses: split horizontally and fill with meats, cheeses, and salads; slice diagonally and toast the slices to serve with soup; or simply cut into chunks, spread with sweet butter and serve with cheese.

5 cups unbleached strong white bread flour

1 cup fine French all-purpose flour

2 teaspoons salt

½ ounce fresh yeast

MAKES THREE LOAVES

1 Sift the flours and salt into a bowl. Add the yeast to 2½ cups lukewarm water in another bowl and stir. Gradually beat in half the flour mixture to form a batter. Cover with plastic wrap and leave for about 3 hours, or until nearly trebled in size.

2 Add the remaining flour, a little at a time, beating with your hand. Turn out onto a lightly floured surface and knead for 8–10 minutes to form a moist dough. Place in a lightly oiled bowl, cover with lightly oiled plastic wrap, and leave to rise, in a warm place, for about 1 hour.

3 Punch down the dough, turn out onto a floured surface, and divide into three equal pieces. Shape each into a ball and then into a 6 x 3 inch rectangle. Fold the bottom third up lengthwise and the top third down and press down. Seal the edges. Repeat two or three more times until each loaf is an oblong. Leave to rest in between folding for a few minutes.

4 Gently stretch each piece of dough into a 13–14-inch long loaf. Pleat a floured dishtowel on a cookie sheet to make three molds for the loaves. Place the loaves between the pleats, cover with lightly oiled plastic wrap, and leave to rise in a warm place for 45–60 minutes.

5 Preheat the oven to maximum, at least 450°F. Roll the loaves onto a cookie sheet, spaced well apart. Slash the top of each loaf diagonally several times. Place at the top of the oven, spray the inside of the oven with water, and bake for 20–25 minutes.

COOK'S TIP Baguettes are difficult to reproduce at home as they require a very hot oven and steam. However, by using less yeast and a triple fermentation you can produce a bread with a superior taste and far better texture than mass-produced baguettes. It also helps if you spray the oven twice with water during the first 5 minutes of baking. These loaves are best eaten on the day of baking.

Rosemary Focaccia

If you do not need both loaves, freeze one for another time and warm it in the oven before serving. Sprinkle the loaves with finely chopped garlic, if you prefer.

MAKES TWO LOAVES

1 Put the flour and yeast in a large bowl with 1 teaspoon salt. Stir in 3 tablespoons of the oil and scant 2 cups lukewarm water. Mix with a round-bladed knife, then by hand to a soft dough, adding a little more lukewarm water if the dough feels dry.

2 Turn the dough out onto a lightly floured surface and knead for 10 minutes, until smooth and elastic. Put in a lightly oiled bowl and cover with oiled plastic wrap. Leave in a warm place for about 1 hour, until doubled in size.

3 Preheat the oven to 400°F. Turn out the dough onto a floured surface and cut in half. Roll out each half into a 10-inch round. Transfer to greased cookie sheets, cover with lightly oiled plastic wrap, and leave for 20 minutes, until risen.

4 Press your fingers into the dough to make deep holes all over it about 1¼ inches apart. Leave for 5 minutes more. Sprinkle with the rosemary and plenty of sea salt. Sprinkle with water to keep the crust moist and bake for 25 minutes, until pale golden. Remove from the oven and drizzle with the remaining olive oil. Transfer to a wire rack to cool.

4 cups strong white bread flour

1 tablespoon rapid-rise dried yeast

5 tablespoons olive oil

3 tablespoons chopped fresh rosemary

Scottish Morning Rolls

These soft, spongy bread rolls are irresistible while still warm and aromatic. Made with milk, rather than the more usual water, they have a rich flavor. In Scotland they are a firm favorite for breakfast with fried eggs and bacon. To speed up the rising time, place the rolls in the airing cupboard or on the top of the preheated oven.

MAKES TEN ROLLS

1 Grease two cookie sheets. Sift the flour and salt together into a large bowl and make a well in the center. Mix the yeast with the milk, then mix in ⅔ cup lukewarm water. Add to the center of the flour and mix together to form a soft dough.

2 Knead the dough lightly in the bowl, then cover with lightly oiled plastic wrap, and leave to rise in a warm place for 1 hour, or until doubled in bulk. Turn the dough out onto a lightly floured surface and punch down.

3 Divide the dough into ten equal pieces. Knead lightly and, using a rolling pin, shape each piece of dough into a flat oval 4 x 3 inches, or a flat round 3½ inches.

4 Transfer to the prepared cookie sheets, spaced well apart, and cover the rolls with oiled plastic wrap. Leave to rise, in a warm place, for about 30 minutes.

5 Meanwhile, preheat the oven to 400°F. Press each roll in the center with the three middle fingers to equalize the air bubbles and to help prevent blistering. Brush with milk and dust with flour. Bake for 15–20 minutes, or until lightly browned. Dust with more flour and cool slightly on a wire rack. Serve warm.

4 cups unbleached strong white bread flour, plus extra for dusting

2 teaspoons salt

¼ ounce fresh yeast

⅔ cup lukewarm milk, plus extra for glazing

Panini all'Olio

Italian-style dough enriched and flavored with extra virgin olive oil is versatile for making decorative rolls. Children will love helping to make and shape these rolls—they can try making twists, fingers, or artichoke-shapes, or just about any shape they want. The rolls are sure to disappear as soon as they are cool enough to eat.

4 cups unbleached strong white bread flour

2 teaspoons salt

½ ounce fresh yeast

4 tablespoons extra virgin olive oil, plus extra for brushing

MAKES SIXTEEN ROLLS

1 Lightly oil three cookie sheets. Sift the flour and salt together in a large bowl and make a well in the center. Measure 1 cup lukewarm water. Cream the yeast with half the water, then stir in the remainder. Add to the well with the oil and mix to a dough.

2 Turn the dough out onto a lightly floured surface and knead for 8–10 minutes, until smooth and elastic. Place in a lightly oiled bowl, cover with lightly oiled plastic wrap, and leave to rise in a warm place for about 1 hour, or until nearly doubled in bulk.

3 Turn the dough onto a lightly floured surface and punch down. Divide into 12 equal pieces and shape into rolls. To make twists, roll each piece of dough into a strip 12 inches long and 1½ inches wide. Twist each strip into a loose spiral and join the ends together to make a circle. Place on the cookie sheets, spaced well apart. Brush lightly with olive oil, cover with lightly oiled plastic wrap, and leave to rise in a warm place for 20–30 minutes.

4 To make fingers, flatten each piece of dough into an oval and roll to about 9 inches long. Roll up from the wider end. Gently stretch the dough roll to 8–9 inches long. Cut in half. Place on the cookie sheets, spaced well apart. Brush the dough with olive oil, cover with lightly oiled plastic wrap, and leave to rise in a warm place for 20–30 minutes.

5 To make artichoke-shapes, shape each piece of dough into a ball and space well apart on the cookie sheets. Brush with oil, cover with lightly oiled plastic wrap, and leave to rise in a warm place for 20–30 minutes. Using scissors, snip ¼-inch deep cuts in a circle on the top of each ball, then make five larger horizontal cuts around the sides.

6 Preheat the oven to 400°F. Bake the rolls for 15 minutes.

Pita Bread

Soft, slightly bubbly pita bread is a pleasure to make. It can be eaten in a variety of ways, such as Mediterranean-style filled with salad or little chunks of meat cooked on the barbecue, or it can be torn into pieces and dipped in savory dips such as hummus or tzatziki. Chop any leftover bread and incorporate into the Lebanese salad *fattoush* with parsley, mint, tomatoes, and cucumber.

MAKES TWELVE

5 cups strong white bread flour, or half white and half whole-wheat

2½ teaspoons rapid-rise dried yeast

1 tablespoon salt

1 tablespoon olive oil

1 Combine the flour, yeast, and salt. Combine the oil and 1 cup water, then add half of the flour mixture, stirring in the same direction, until the dough is stiff. Knead in the remaining flour. Place the dough in a clean bowl, cover with a clean dishtowel, and leave in a warm place for at least 30 minutes and up to 2 hours.

2 Knead the dough for 10 minutes, or until smooth. Lightly oil the bowl, place the dough in it, cover again, and leave to rise in a warm place for about 1 hour, or until doubled in size.

3 Divide the dough into 12 equal pieces. With lightly floured hands, flatten each piece, then roll out into a round measuring about 8 inches and about ¼–½ inch thick. Keep the rolled breads covered while you make the remaining pitas.

4 Heat a heavy skillet over medium-high heat. When hot, lay one piece of flattened dough in the skillet and cook for 15–20 seconds. Turn it over and cook the second side for about 1 minute.

5 When large bubbles start to form on the bread, turn it over again. It should puff up. Using a clean dishtowel, gently press on the bread where the bubbles have formed. Cook for a total of 3 minutes, then remove the pita from the skillet. Repeat with the remaining dough. Wrap the pita breads in a clean dishtowel, stacking them as each one is cooked. Serve the pitas hot while they are soft and moist.

VARIATION

To bake the breads, preheat the oven to 425°F. Fill an unglazed or partially glazed dish with hot water and place in the bottom of the hot oven. Alternatively, arrange a handful of unglazed tiles in the base of the oven. Use either a nonstick cookie sheet or a lightly oiled cookie sheet and heat in the oven for a few minutes. Place two or three pieces of flattened dough onto the hot cookie sheet and place in the hottest part of the oven. Bake for 2–3 minutes, until puffed up. Repeat with the remaining dough.

Yemeni Sponge Flat Breads

These flat breads, known as *lahuhs* and made from a batter, are bubbly and soft. They are eaten with soups but are also good with salads, dips, or cheese.

SERVES FOUR

1 Measure generous 2 cups lukewarm water. In a bowl, dissolve the dried yeast in about 5 tablespoons of the water. Leave in a warm place for about 10 minutes, or until frothy.

2 Stir the remaining water, the flour, salt, and melted butter or vegetable oil into the yeast mixture and mix until it forms a smooth batter. Cover with a clean dishtowel, then leave in a warm place for about 1 hour, until doubled in size.

3 Stir the thick, frothy batter and, if it seems too thick to ladle out, add a little extra water. Cover and leave the batter to stand in a warm place for about 1 hour.

4 Cook the flat breads in a nonstick skillet. Ladle 3–4 tablespoons of batter (or less for smaller breads) into the skillet and cook over low heat until the top is bubbling and the color has changed. (Traditionally these breads are cooked on only one side, but they can be turned over and the second side cooked for just a moment, if you like.)

5 Remove the cooked flat bread from the skillet with a spatula and keep warm in a clean dishtowel. Continue cooking until you have used up all the remaining batter.

1 tablespoons dried active yeast

3 cups all-purpose flour

1 teaspoon salt

¼ cup butter, melted, or 4 tablespoons vegetable oil

COOK'S TIP *Use two or three heavy skillets at the same time so that the flat breads are ready together and so can be eaten piping hot.*

West Indian Flat Breads

Eclectic Caribbean food is influenced by a wide range of international cultures. It is the Anglo-Indian connection that brought the Indian flat bread called roti to Trinidad in the West Indies. Serve these simple-to-make breads straight from the pan to accompany spicy seafood chowders, curries, or any other dish that has plenty of sauce for mopping up.

MAKES EIGHT ROTIS

1 Mix the flour, baking powder, and salt together in a large bowl and make a well in the center. Gradually mix in 1¼ cups water to make a firm dough.

2 Knead on a lightly floured surface until smooth. Place in a lightly oiled bowl and cover with lightly oiled plastic wrap. Let stand for 20 minutes.

3 Divide the dough into eight equal pieces and roll each one on a lightly floured surface into a 7-inch round. Brush the surface of each round with a little of the clarified butter or ghee, fold in half, and then in half again. Cover the folded rounds with lightly oiled plastic wrap and leave for 10 minutes.

4 Take one roti and roll out on a lightly floured surface into a round about 8–9 inches in diameter. Brush both sides with some clarified butter or ghee.

5 Heat a griddle or heavy skillet, add the roti, and cook for about 1 minute. Turn over and cook for 2 minutes, then turn over again, and cook for 1 minute. Wrap in a clean dishtowel to keep warm while cooking the remaining rotis. Serve warm.

4 cups atta or fine whole-wheat flour

1 teaspoon baking powder

1 teaspoon salt

8–10 tablespoons clarified butter or ghee, melted

Tandoori Rotis

Indian flat breads are fun to make at home: These may not be strictly authentic in terms of cooking method, but they taste fantastic. This bread would normally be baked in a tandoor, a clay oven that is heated with charcoal or wood. The oven becomes extremely hot, cooking the bread in minutes. The rotis are ready when light brown bubbles appear on the surface.

MAKES SIX ROTIS

3 cups atta or fine whole-wheat flour

1 teaspoon salt

2–3 tablespoons melted ghee or butter, for brushing

1 Sift the flour and salt into a large bowl. Add 1 cup water and mix to a soft dough. Knead on a lightly floured surface for 3–4 minutes, until smooth. Place the dough in a lightly oiled mixing bowl, cover with lightly oiled plastic wrap, and leave to rest for 1 hour.

2 Turn out onto a lightly floured surface. Divide the dough into six pieces and shape each piece into a ball. Press out into a larger round with the palm of your hand, cover with lightly oiled plastic wrap, and leave to rest for 10 minutes.

3 Meanwhile, preheat the oven to 450°F. Place three cookie sheets in the oven to heat. Roll the rotis into 6-inch rounds, place two on each cookie sheet and bake for 8–10 minutes. Brush with ghee or butter and serve warm.

Preserves, Pickles, Relishes and Sauces

SWEET AND SAVORY PRESERVES, CONDIMENTS AND

SAUCES CAN ADD THE FINISHING TOUCH TO A SIMPLE DISH.

A SPOONFUL OF FRUIT JAM OR JELLY CAN TRANSFORM A

PLAIN SCONE INTO TEATIME TREAT, WHILE PIQUANT PICKLES

AND RELISHES CAN ENLIVEN BREAD AND CHEESE, AND A

FLAVORSOME SAUCE CAN TURN SIMPLY COOKED FISH INTO

A REALLY SPECIAL MEAL.

Bramble Jelly

The sharp, fruity flavor of wild blackberries makes this jelly one of the best, especially for serving with hot buttered toast or English muffins. When picking the fruit, include a small proportion of red unripe berries for a good set. Red currant jelly can be made in exactly the same way, but with less sugar. Reduce the quantity to 1½ cups of sugar for every 2½ cups of fruit juice.

8 cups blackberries

juice of 1 lemon

about 4 cups superfine sugar

MAKES 2 POUNDS

1 Put the blackberries and lemon juice into a large pan (use a preserving pan with two handles if possible). Add 1¼ cups water. Cover the pan and cook for 15–30 minutes, or until the blackberries are very soft.

2 Ladle into a jelly bag or a large strainer lined with cheesecloth and set over a large mixing bowl. Leave the fruit to drip overnight to obtain the maximum amount of juice. Do not disturb or squeeze the bag or the jelly will be cloudy.

3 Discard the fruit pulp. Measure the juice and allow 2 cups sugar to every 2½ cups juice. Place the juice and sugar in a large, heavy pan and bring to a boil, stirring constantly until the sugar has dissolved.

4 Boil the mixture rapidly until the jelly registers 220°F on a sugar thermometer, or test for setting by spooning a small amount onto a chilled saucer (keep a saucer in the freezer for this purpose). Chill for 3 minutes, then push the mixture with your finger: if wrinkles form on the surface of the jelly, it is ready.

5 Skim off any scum and immediately pour the jelly into warm sterilized jars. Cover and seal immediately, then label when the jars are cold.

Strawberry Preserve

This is the classic fragrant preserve for traditional English afternoon tea, served with freshly baked biscuits and clotted cream. It is also extremely good stirred into plain yogurt for breakfast. When choosing strawberries for making preserves, pick undamaged, slightly underripe fruit if possible—the pectin content will be high and insure a good set.

8 cups small strawberries

4 cups granulated sugar

juice of 2 lemons

MAKES ABOUT 3 POUNDS

1 Layer the strawberries and sugar in a large bowl. Cover and leave overnight.

2 The next day, scrape the strawberries and their juice into a large, heavy pan. Add the lemon juice. Gradually bring to a boil over low heat, stirring until the sugar has dissolved.

3 Boil steadily for 10–15 minutes, or until the preserve registers 220°F on a sugar thermometer. Alternatively, test for setting by spooning a small amount onto a chilled saucer. Chill for 3 minutes, then push the preserve with your finger: if wrinkles form on the surface, it is ready. Let cool for about 10 minutes.

4 Stir the preserve before pouring it into warm sterilized jars, filling them right to the top. Cover with waxed paper disks at once, but do not seal with lids until the preserve is completely cold.

COOK'S TIP *For best results when making preserves, don't wash the strawberries unless absolutely necessary. Instead, brush off any dirt, or wipe the strawberries with a damp cloth. If you have to wash any, pat them dry and then spread them out on a clean dishtowel.*

Spiced Poached Kumquats

Warm cinnamon and star anise make a heady combination with the full citrus flavor of kumquats. Star anise is an attractive spice: it is an eight-pointed star that contains tiny aniseed-flavored, amber colored seeds. The kumquats go well with rich meats, such as roast pork or baked cured ham, or with punchy goat milk cheese. They are also good with desserts and ice creams.

SERVES SIX

1 Cut the kumquats in half and discard the seeds. Place the kumquats in a pan with the superfine sugar, ⅔ cup water, and the cinnamon stick and star anise. Cook over gentle heat, stirring until the sugar has dissolved.

2 Increase the heat, cover the pan, and boil the mixture for about 8–10 minutes, until the kumquats are tender. To bottle the kumquats, spoon them into warm, sterilized jars, seal, and label.

3 If you want to serve the spiced kumquats soon after making them, let the mixture cool, then chill it.

4 cups kumquats

½ cup superfine sugar

1 small cinnamon stick

1 star anise

Three-fruit Marmalade

Bitter marmalade oranges have a powerful flavor and plenty of setting power to make an excellent preserve. Known as Temple oranges, they are usually only available for a short time in January—but sweet oranges can be used in this recipe if necessary.

MAKES 5 POUNDS

1 Wash the fruit, halve, and squeeze their juice. Pour into a large heavy pan or preserving pan. Tip the seeds and pulp into a square of cheesecloth, gather the sides into a bag, and tie the neck. Tie the bag to the pan handle so that it dangles in the juice.

2 Remove and discard the membranes and pith from the citrus skins and cut the rinds into slivers. Add to the pan with 7½ cups water. Heat until simmering and then cook gently for 2 hours. Test the rinds for softness by pressing a cooled piece with a finger.

3 Lift out the cheesecloth bag, squeezing out the juice into the pan. Stir the sugar into the pan and heat very gently, stirring occasionally, until the sugar has dissolved.

4 Bring the mixture to a boil and boil for 10–15 minutes, or until the marmalade registers 220°F on a sugar thermometer. Alternatively, test the marmalade for setting by pouring a small amount onto a chilled saucer. Chill for 3 minutes, then push the marmalade with your finger: if wrinkles form on the surface, it is ready. Cool for 15 minutes.

5 Stir the marmalade and pour it into warm, sterilized jars. Cover with waxed paper disks. Seal and label when completely cold. Store in a cool dark pantry.

2 Temple oranges

2 lemons

1 grapefruit

6¾ cups granulated sugar

COOK'S TIP *Let the marmalade to cool slightly before potting so that it is thick enough to stop the fruit from sinking in the jars.*

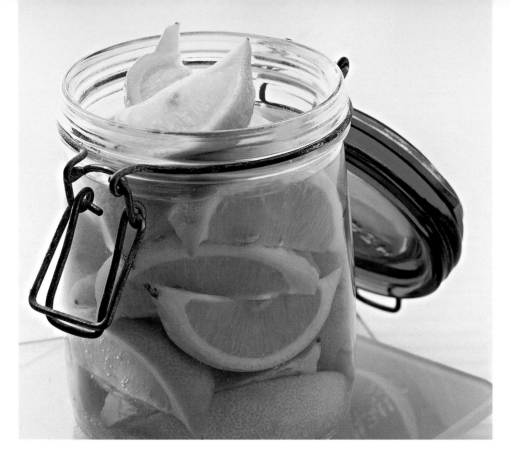

Preserved Lemons

These are widely used in Middle Eastern cooking, for which only the peel is used and not the pulp. In this recipe, the lemons are cut into wedges instead of being preserved whole, in traditional style. The wedges are more practical for potting and they are also easy to prepare before use.

MAKES TWO JARS

1 Wash the lemons well and cut each into six to eight wedges. Press a generous amount of sea salt into the cut surfaces, pushing it into every crevice.

2 Pack the salted lemon wedges into two 5-cup sterilized jars. To each jar, add 2–3 tablespoons salt and 6 tablespoons lemon juice, then top off with boiling water to cover the lemons. (If using larger jars, use more lemon juice and less water.)

3 Cover the jars and let stand for 2–4 weeks before serving.

4 To serve, rinse the preserved lemons well to remove some of the salty flavor, then pull off, and discard the flesh. Cut the lemon peel into strips or leave in chunks and use as you like.

10 unwaxed lemons

about scant 1 cup fresh lemon juice or a combination of fresh and preserved

sea salt

Middle Eastern Pickle

Beets brings attractive color and its inimitable sweet, slightly earthy flavor to this Middle Eastern specialty. The pickle is delicious with falafel or cold roast beef. When buying beets, choose firm, unblemished, small- to medium-size specimens. If you buy beets with green tops, reserve them and cook like spinach for a tasty vegetable accompaniment.

MAKES FOUR JARS

**2¼ pounds
young turnips**

3–4 raw beets

**about 3 tablespoons
kosher salt or
coarse sea salt**

juice of 1 lemon

1 Wash, but do not peel the turnips and beets. Then cut them into slices about ¼ inch thick. Put the salt in a bowl with about 6¼ cups water, stir, and set aside until the salt has completely dissolved.

2 Sprinkle the beets with lemon juice and divide among four 5-cup sterilized jars. Top with the sliced turnips, packing them in very tightly. Pour over the brine, making sure that the vegetables are completely covered.

3 Seal the jars and leave in a cool place for 7 days for the flavors to develop before serving.

Horseradish and Beet Sauce

This is a traditional Jewish specialty. Known as *chrain*, it is often eaten at Pesah, the Passover meal, for which horseradish is one of the traditional bitter flavors. However, it complements a variety of foods and dishes of many different cooking styles, including roast meats and broiled fish.

SERVES ABOUT EIGHT

5 ounces grated fresh horseradish

2 cooked beets, grated

1 tablespoon sugar

1–2 tablespoons red wine vinegar

1 Put the horseradish and beets in a bowl and mix together, then season with sugar, vinegar, and salt to taste.

2 Spoon the sauce into a sterilized jar, packing it down firmly, and seal. Store in the refrigerator, where it will keep for up to 2 weeks.

COOK'S TIP *Fresh horseradish is very potent and should be handled with care as it can make the skin burn as well as the eyes run. Wear fine latex gloves to protect your hands and always work in a well-ventilated kitchen.*

Yellow Bell Pepper and Cilantro Relish

Relishes are quick and easy to make and they are delicious with cold meats and cheese or as a sandwich filler. Here the ingredients are lightly cooked, then processed to a chunky consistency. Red or orange bell peppers will work just as well as yellow, as they all have a sweet flavor. Don't use green bell peppers though, because they are not sweet.

SERVES FOUR TO SIX

1 Seed and coarsely chop the bell peppers. Heat the oil in a skillet and gently cook the bell peppers, stirring frequently, for about 8–10 minutes, until lightly colored.

2 Meanwhile, seed the chile and slice it as thinly as possible. Transfer the bell peppers and cooking juices to a food processor and process lightly until chopped. Transfer half the bell peppers to a bowl. Using a sharp knife, chop the cilantro, then add to the processor and process briefly.

3 Tip the contents of the food processor into the bowl with the rest of the bell peppers and add the chile and salt. Mix well, cover, and chill until ready to serve.

3 large yellow bell peppers

3 tablespoons sesame oil

1 large mild fresh red chile

small handful of fresh cilantro

COOK'S TIP *Other flavored oils, such as lemon- or garlic-steeped oil, can be used in place of the sesame oil. The relish can be stored in an airtight container in the refrigerator for several days.*

Hot Mango Salsa

For sweet, tangy results, select a really juicy, ripe mango for this salsa—it is not worth making the salsa with a firm, unripe mango as it will not taste so good as it should. Keep an unripe mango in the fruit bowl for a few days until it has ripened. This fruity salsa is a delicious accompaniment to broiled chicken or fish or foods cooked on the barbecue.

SERVES FOUR TO SIX

1 To prepare the mango, cut the flesh off on either side of the flat pit. Peel and finely dice the mango halves and cut off and chop the flesh that still clings to the pit.

2 Finely grate the lime rind and squeeze the juice. Seed and finely shred the fresh red chile.

3 Finely chop the onion and mix it in a bowl with the mango, lime rind, 1 tablespoon lime juice, the chile, and a little salt. Cover and chill until ready to serve.

1 medium ripe mango

1 lime

1 large mild fresh red chile

½ small red onion

Harissa

This simplified version of harissa—the classic spicy North African sauce—is extremely quick to make. It can be served as a dip with wedges of Middle Eastern flat bread, as a condiment with couscous and other North African dishes, or as a flavoring to spice up meat and vegetable stews. This basic spice blend goes very well with other aromatic herbs and spices so you can vary the flavor by adding chopped fresh cilantro or a pinch of caraway seeds along with the lemon juice, if you like.

SERVES FOUR TO SIX

1 Put the paprika, cayenne pepper, ground cumin and 1 cup water in a large, heavy pan and season with salt to taste.

2 Bring the spice mixture to a boil, then immediately remove the pan from the heat.

3 Stir in the lemon juice to taste and and let cool completely before serving or using.

3 tablespoons paprika

½–1 teaspoon cayenne pepper

¼ teaspoon ground cumin

juice of ¼–½ lemon

Aioli

This classic, creamy garlic mayonnaise from France is simple to make and absolutely delicious. Serve it with salads or as a dip with crudités, with potato wedges, or as a quick sauce for pan-fried salmon. Try to use extra virgin olive oil for this mayonnaise if you can—it has a rich and delicious flavor that really makes this sauce special.

SERVES FOUR TO SIX

1 Put the garlic cloves in a mortar, add a pinch of salt, and pound to a smooth paste with a pestle.

2 Transfer the garlic paste to a bowl. Add the egg yolks and whisk for about 30 seconds, until creamy. Whisk in the olive oil, drop by drop, until the mixture begins to thicken, then add the oil in a slow drizzle until the mixture is thick and creamy.

3 Beat in the lemon juice and seasoning to taste. Serve the aioli immediately or cover with plastic wrap and chill in the refrigerator until ready to use. Let the aioli return to room temperature for 30 minutes before serving.

4 large garlic cloves, peeled

2 egg yolks

1 cup extra virgin olive oil

1–2 tablespoons lemon juice

Roasted Garlic Sauce

A roasted garlic sauce has plenty of robust flavor without the harshness of some uncooked garlic sauces and dressings. This one keeps well in the refrigerator for several days. Serve it as an accompaniment to burgers or sausages cooked on the barbecue, broiled steaks, lamb chops, or pork steaks—the possibilities are endless.

6 large heads of garlic

½ cup extra virgin olive oil

2 thick slices white bread, about 3½ ounces

2–3 tablespoons lemon juice

SERVES SIX TO EIGHT

1 Preheat the oven to 400°F. Slice the tops off the garlic and place the bulbs on a sheet of foil. Spoon over 2 tablespoons of the oil and sprinkle with salt. Wrap the foil over the garlic and bake for 1 hour, until soft. Open out the foil and let the garlic cool.

2 Discard the crusts from the bread. Soak the bread in water for 1 minute, then squeeze dry, and place in a food processor. Squeeze the garlic flesh into the processor. Process to a smooth paste.

3 Add 2 tablespoons lemon juice with a little salt and pepper. With the machine running, gradually add the remaining oil in a thin stream to make a smooth paste. Check the seasoning, adding more lemon juice if needed. Turn into a bowl, cover, and chill until required.

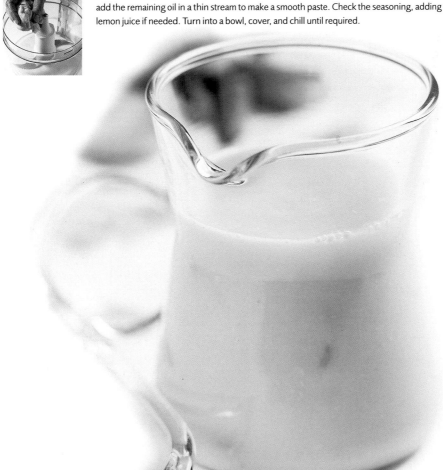

Watercress Sauce

This pretty green sauce is refreshingly sharp and peppery. It is delicious served as an accompaniment to poached fish, or as a dip for simply broiled shrimp. Do not prepare the sauce more than a few hours ahead of serving, as the watercress will discolor the sauce. This peppery green sauce can also be made with arugula leaves instead of the watercress.

SERVES SIX TO EIGHT

7 ounces watercress leaves

11 ounces mayonnaise

1–2 tablespoons freshly squeezed lemon juice

scant 1 cup sweet butter

1 Remove the tough stems from the watercress leaves and finely chop the leaves by hand or in a food processor. Add the mayonnaise and the freshly squeezed lemon juice and process to mix.

2 Melt the sweet butter, then add to the watercress mixture, a little at a time, processing or whisking in a bowl until the butter has been fully incorporated and the sauce is thick and smooth. Season to taste with salt and pepper, then cover, and chill in the refrigerator for at least an hour before serving.

EXTRAS *Garlic makes a delicious addition to this sauce. Peel and finely chop 1–2 garlic cloves and combine with the chopped watercress leaves, mayonnaise, and lemon juice, before adding the melted butter in step 2.*

Shallots in Balsamic Vinegar

These whole shallots cooked in balsamic vinegar and herbs are a modern variation on pickled onions, but they have a much gentler, smoother flavor. They are delicious served with cold pies, meats, and cheese. A combination of bay leaves and thyme is used here, but rosemary, oregano, or marjoram sprigs would work just as well.

SERVES SIX

1 Put the unpeeled shallots in a bowl, cover with boiling water, and leave for 2 minutes for the skins to loosen. Drain and peel the shallots, leaving them whole.

2 Put the sugar, bay leaves or thyme, and vinegar in a heavy pan and bring to a boil. Add the shallots, cover, and simmer gently for about 40 minutes, until the shallots are just tender.

3 Transfer the mixture to a sterilized jar, seal, and label, then store in a cool, dark place. Alternatively, drain and transfer to a serving dish. Let cool, then chill until ready to serve.

1¼ pounds shallots

2 tablespoons molasses sugar

several bay leaves or fresh thyme sprigs

1¼ cups balsamic vinegar

Barbecue Sauce

A wide selection of ready-made barbecue sauces is available in the supermarkets, but they really don't compare with the homemade variety. This 10-minute version can be used to transform baked or broiled chicken, sausages, or fish into an interesting meal that needs no more than a mixed salad and baked potatoes as accompaniments.

SERVES FOUR TO SIX

1 Tip the cans of chopped tomatoes with herbs or garlic into a medium, heavy pan and add the finely chopped onion, molasses, and Worcestershire sauce.

2 Bring to a boil and cook, uncovered, until the mixture is thickened and pulpy, stirring frequently with a wooden spoon to stop the sauce catching on the base of the pan. Season lightly with salt and plenty of freshly ground black pepper and transfer to a serving dish or pitcher. Serve the sauce warm or cold.

2 x 14-ounce cans chopped tomatoes with herbs or garlic

1 onion, finely chopped

1 tablespoon molasses

3 tablespoons Worcestershire sauce

Mixed Herb and Peppercorn Sauce

This lovely, refreshing sauce relies on absolutely fresh herbs (any combination will do) and good-quality olive oil for its fabulous flavor. Make it a day in advance to let the flavors mingle. Serve the sauce with simply cooked fish, such as salmon, or with broiled beef or lamb steaks.

SERVES FOUR TO SIX

1 Crush the cumin seeds using a mortar and pestle. Alternatively, put the seeds in a small bowl and pound them with the end of a rolling pin. Add the pink or green peppercorns and pound a little to break them up slightly.

2 Remove any tough stalks from the herbs. Put the herbs in a food processor with the cumin seeds, peppercorns, oil, and salt and process until the herbs are finely chopped, scraping the sauce down from the sides of the bowl if necessary.

3 Turn the sauce into a small serving dish, cover with plastic wrap, and chill until ready to serve.

2 teaspoons cumin seeds

1 tablespoon pink or green peppercorns in brine, drained and rinsed

1 cup fresh mixed herbs, such as parsley, mint, chives, and cilantro

3 tablespoons lemon-steeped olive oil

Index

NOTES

Notes

NOTES

NOTES

NOTES

NOTES

NOTES

NOTES